Introduction

Welcome to "Air Fryer Baking Cookbook for Beginners," your essential guide to the delightful world of air fryer baking. As a professional baker, I have spent countless hours in kitchens, experimenting with recipes, ingredients, and techniques. My journey has led me to a wonderful discovery: the air fryer, a versatile and convenient tool that transforms traditional baking into an easier, healthier, and more accessible experience for everyone.

Baking, for many, is not just about creating something delicious; it's an art form, a therapeutic process, and a way to express love and creativity. However, the idea of baking can be daunting, especially for beginners. The fear of complicated methods, the mess of endless utensils, and the challenge of mastering temperatures and timings often keep many from exploring the joy of baking. This is where "Air Fryer Baking Cookbook for Beginners" comes in, offering a perfect solution.

In this book, you will find over 180 simple and delightful baking recipes, ranging from classic cakes and brownies to innovative cookies, pies, muffins, tarts, and more. Each recipe has been meticulously crafted to ensure simplicity without compromising on taste or quality.

This cookbook is designed for everyone: from those taking their first steps in baking to seasoned bakers seeking to explore the potential of air fryer baking. It is more than just a collection of recipes; it's a journey through the joys of baking with tips, tricks, and insights to enhance your baking experience. Whether you're looking to satisfy a sweet craving, preparing treats for a gathering, or simply exploring new ways to bake, this book will guide you through each step with ease and confidence.

So, preheat your air fryer, gather your ingredients, and get ready to embark on an exciting baking adventure. Let's create something extraordinary together!

With warmth and whisk in hand,

TOP TIPS FOR BEGINNERS USE AIR FRYER

- **Read the Manual:** Always start by reading the user manual that comes with your specific air fryer model. This will help you understand the features, settings, and safety guidelines.
- **Preheat the Air Fryer:** Preheating your air fryer before cooking can help achieve better results. It usually takes around 3-5 minutes to preheat.
- **Use a Light Coat of Oil:** One of the advantages of air frying is that it requires less oil than traditional frying. Use a cooking spray or a small amount of oil to lightly coat the food for a crispy texture.
- **Avoid Overcrowding:** For even cooking, avoid overcrowding the air fryer basket. Give enough space between the food items to allow hot air to circulate freely.
- **Shake or Flip Midway:** To ensure that your food cooks evenly, shake the basket or flip the items halfway through the cooking time. This is especially important for items like French fries or chicken wings.
- **Experiment with Temperature and Time:** Air fryers have different temperature settings and cooking times. Experiment with these settings to find what works best for different types of food. Refer to the cooking chart in the manual as a starting point.
- **Use Parchment Paper or Basket Liners:** To make cleanup easier and prevent sticking, consider using parchment paper or basket liners. Make sure they are rated for use in air fryers and can withstand high temperatures.
- **Check for Doneness:** Always check the internal temperature of meat to ensure it's cooked thoroughly. The recommended internal temperatures for various meats are widely available and should be followed for safety.
- **Prep Food Properly:** Pat food items dry before placing them in the air fryer. Excess moisture can affect the crispiness of the final result. Season your food before placing it in the air fryer for better flavor.
- **Get Creative:** Don't limit yourself to traditional fried foods. Experiment with a variety of recipes, from vegetables and proteins to desserts. The air fryer is versatile and can be used for a wide range of dishes.
- **Clean Regularly:** Regularly clean your air fryer to maintain its performance and prevent any lingering odors. Most air fryers have parts that are dishwasher safe, making cleanup convenient.
- **Be Patient:** Cooking times can vary based on the air fryer model and the type of food. Be patient and use trial and error to determine the optimal cooking times for your favorite recipes.

CLEAN YOUR AIR FRYER PROPERLY

Cleaning your air fryer properly is essential for maintaining its performance and ensuring the longevity of the appliance. Here's a step-by-step guide on how to clean your air fryer:

- **Unplug the Air Fryer:** Before starting the cleaning process, make sure the air fryer is unplugged and has cooled down to a safe temperature.

- **Remove Removable Parts:** Take out the basket, tray, and any other removable parts from the air fryer. Check the user manual to identify all the removable components.

- **Dispose of Excess Oil:** If there is excess oil or grease in the bottom of the fryer, carefully dispose of it. You can pour it into a container and discard it or save it for later use.

- **Soak Removable Parts:** Soak the removable parts, such as the basket and tray, in warm, soapy water. This will help loosen any stuck-on food particles. Use a soft sponge or brush to gently scrub away any residue.

- **Clean the Interior:** Wipe down the interior of the air fryer with a damp cloth or sponge. Be gentle and avoid using abrasive materials that could damage the non-stick coating.

- **Clean the Heating Element:** If your air fryer has a visible heating element, use a soft brush or cloth to remove any debris. Do this carefully to avoid damaging the heating element.

- **Clean the Exterior:** Wipe down the exterior of the air fryer with a damp cloth. If there are stubborn stains, you can use a mild kitchen cleaner, but avoid getting any cleaning solutions on the heating element or electrical components.

- **Check the Vent:** Ensure that the air vents are clear of any obstructions. Use a brush or compressed air to remove any dust or debris from the vents.

- **Clean the Heating Element Cover (if applicable):** Some air fryers have a heating element cover. Refer to the user manual for instructions on cleaning it. If it's removable, clean it according to the manual's guidelines.

- **Dry Thoroughly:** After cleaning, thoroughly dry all the parts before reassembling the air fryer. This helps prevent any water from affecting the appliance's performance.

- **Reassemble:** Once everything is clean and dry, reassemble the air fryer by putting the removable parts back in place.

- **Store Properly:** Store your air fryer in a cool, dry place when not in use. Make sure it's protected from dust and other contaminants.

BAKING CONVERSION CHART

DRY INGREDIENTS

Ingredient	Cups	Grams (g)	Ounces (oz)
All-Purpose Flour	1 cup	125 g	4.4 oz
Granulated Sugar	1 cup	200 g	7.1 oz
Brown Sugar (packed)	1 cup	220 g	7.8 oz
Powdered Sugar	1 cup	125 g	4.4 oz
Cocoa Powder	1 cup	85 g	3 oz
Nuts (chopped)	1 cup	115 g	4 oz
Butter	1 cup	227 g	8 oz

LIQUID INGREDIENTS

Ingredient	Cups	Milliliters (ml)	Fluid Ounces (fl oz)
Water	1 cup	240 ml	8 fl oz
Milk	1 cup	240 ml	8 fl oz
Buttermilk	1 cup	240 ml	8 fl oz
Vegetable Oil	1 cup	240 ml	8 fl oz
Honey	1 cup	340 g	12 fl oz
Maple Syrup	1 cup	320 g	11.3 fl oz

AIR FRYER TEMP

Celsius	100°C	110°C	120°C	140°C	150°C	160°C	175°C	180°C	200°C	220°C	240°C
Fahrenheit	212°F	230°F	248°F	284°F	302°F	320°F	347°F	356°F	392°F	428°F	464°F

TABLE OF CONTENTS

Pie & Tart

- Fish Pies — 1
- Cottage Pies — 1
- Pumpkin Pies — 2
- Ratatouille Pies — 2
- Chicken Korma Pies — 3
- Pork and Sage Pies — 3
- Caramel Apple Pies — 4
- Chocolate Silk Pies — 4
- Lemon Meringue Pies — 5
- Rabbit and Leek Pies — 5
- Leek and Potato Pies — 6
- Pear and Ginger Pies — 6
- Thai Green Curry Pies — 7
- Potato and Cheese Pies — 7
- Chicken and Pesto Pies — 8
- Sausage and Apple Pies — 8
- Turkey and Stuffing Pies — 9
- Guinness and Onion Pies — 9
- Beef and Horseradish Pies — 10
- Chicken and Mushroom Pies — 10
- Mocha Tarts — 11
- Caprese Tarts — 11
- Key Lime Tarts — 12
- Blackberry Tarts — 12
- Maple Pecan Tarts — 13
- Ratatouille Tarts — 13
- Blood Orange Tarts — 14
- Black Forest Tarts — 14
- Cherry Almond Tarts — 15
- Raspberry Rose Tarts — 15
- Cinnamon Apple Tarts — 16
- Feta and Olive Tarts — 16
- Cherry Bakewell Tarts — 17
- Plum and Ginger Tarts — 17
- Chocolate Orange Tarts — 18
- Chocolate Mousse Tarts — 18
- Lemon Blackberry Tarts — 19
- Coffee and Walnut Tarts — 19
- Orange and Cardamom Tarts — 20
- Blueberry Cheesecake Tarts — 20

Cakes

- Mocha Cake — 21
- Coffee Cake — 21
- Coconut Cake — 22
- Snickers Cake — 22
- Pecan Pie Cake — 23
- Red Velvet Cake — 23
- Hummingbird Cake — 24
- Key Lime Pie Cake — 24
- Pumpkin Spice Cake — 25
- Vanilla Pound Cake — 25
- Earl Grey Tea Cake — 26
- Pumpkin Cake — 26
- Pistachio Rose Cake — 27
- Apple Cinnamon Cake — 27
- Chocolate Mint Cake — 28
- Banana Nutella Cake — 28
- Rhubarb Crumble Cake — 29
- Victoria Sponge Cake — 29
- Blueberry Lemon Cake — 30
- Hazelnut Praline Cake — 30
- Raspberry Cake — 31
- Hazelnut Cake — 31
- Raspberry Ripple Cake — 32
- Lemon Poppy Seed Cake — 32
- Chocolate Cherry Cake — 33
- Saffron and Honey Cake — 33
- Mango and Coconut Cake — 34
- Chocolate Hazelnut Cake — 34
- Mint Chocolate Chip Cake — 35

TABLE OF CONTENTS

- Coconut Mango Bundt Cake — 35
- Pistachio Cranberry Cake — 36
- Chocolate Raspberry Cake — 36
- Ginger Molasses Cake — 37
- Lemon Elderflower Cake — 37
- Chocolate Zucchini Cake — 38
- Red Wine Chocolate Cake — 38

Muffins

- Hazelnut Muffins — 39
- Earl Grey Muffins — 39
- Almond Joy Muffins — 40
- Gingerbread Muffins — 40
- Maple Bacon Muffins — 41
- Apple Cider Muffins — 41
- Apple Walnut Muffins — 42
- Maple Walnut Muffins — 42
- Mango Banana Muffins — 43
- Orange Ginger Muffins — 43
- Peach Cobbler Muffins — 44
- Mango Coconut Muffins — 44
- Pumpkin Pecan Muffins — 45
- Caramel Pecan Muffins — 45
- Apricot Almond Muffins — 46
- Apple Streusel Muffins — 46
- Chocolate Mint Muffins — 47
- Honey Cornbread Muffins — 47
- Raspberry Swirl Muffins — 48
- Ginger Molasses Muffins — 48
- Chocolate Orange Muffins — 49
- Cranberry Walnut Muffins — 49
- Chocolate Cherry Muffins — 50
- Coconut Raspberry Muffins — 50
- Strawberry Banana Muffins — 51
- Chocolate Zucchini Muffins — 51
- Blackberry Vanilla Muffins — 52
- Strawberry Rhubarb Muffins — 52
- Cranberry Pistachio Muffins — 53
- Blueberry Cheesecake Muffins — 53
- Mocha Chocolate Chip Muffins — 54
- Cherry Chocolate Chip Muffins — 54

Cookies

- Sugar Cookies — 55
- Pecan Sandies — 55
- Linzer Cookies — 56
- Anzac Biscuits — 56
- Funfetti Cookies — 57
- Trail Mix Cookies — 57
- Shortbread Cookies — 58
- Gingerbread Cookies — 58
- Maple Pecan Cookies — 59
- Maple Bacon Cookies — 59
- Toffee Pecan Cookies — 60
- Coconut Lime Cookies — 60
- Macadamia Nut Cookies — 61
- Peanut Butter Cookies — 61
- Almond Butter Cookies — 62
- Bourbon Pecan Cookies — 62
- Apple Cinnamon Cookies — 63
- Mocha Hazelnut Cookies — 63
- Fig and Walnut Biscuits — 64
- Apricot Coconut Cookies — 64
- Double Chocolate Cookies — 65
- Lemon Shortbread Cookies — 65
- Cranberry Orange Cookies — 66
- Espresso Walnut Biscuits — 66
- Chocolate Crinkle Cookies — 67
- Raspberry Jam Thumbprints — 67
- Lemon Lavender Shortbread — 68
- Raspberry Thumbprint Cookies — 68

TABLE OF CONTENTS

Breads

- Chapati — 69
- Flatbread — 69
- Naan Bread — 70
- Pita Bread — 70
- Herb Knots — 71
- Seed bread — 71
- Onion Bread — 72
- Garlic Bread — 72
- Garlic Knots — 73
- Rustic Bread — 73
- Potato Bread — 74
- Cheese Twists — 74
- Pretzel Bites — 75
- Artisan Bread — 75
- Sourdough Discs — 76
- British Twist — 76
- Cinnamon Swirl Bread — 77
- Hemp seed Bread — 77
- Spelt Flour Buns — 78
- Pizza Dough Bites — 78
- Buttery Soft Rolls — 79
- Tomato Basil Flatbread — 79
- Cheese and Herb Focaccia — 80
- Cinnamon Sugar Flatbread — 80
- Fruit and Nut Bread Slices — 81
- Olive and Rosemary Focaccia — 81

Donuts

- Mint Julep Donuts — 82
- Lemon Zest Donuts — 82
- Rum Raisin Donuts — 83
- Gingerbread Donuts — 83
- Coconut Lime Donuts — 84
- Cherry Almond Donuts — 84
- Caramel Pecan Donuts — 85
- Mango Coconut Donuts — 85
- Pecan Praline Donuts — 86
- Bourbon Pecan Pie Donuts — 86
- Chocolate Mint Donuts — 87
- Banana Caramel Donuts — 87
- Blueberry Almond Donuts — 88
- Blackberry Jelly Donuts — 88
- Cranberry Walnut Donuts — 89
- Chocolate Coconut Donuts — 89
- Coconut Rum Glazed Donuts — 90
- Toffee Pecan Donuts — 90
- Passion Fruit Glazed Donuts — 91
- Pumpkin Spice Latte Donuts — 91
- Mint Chocolate Chip Donuts — 92
- Butterscotch Glazed Donuts — 92

Fish Pies

Prep: 20 Min | Cook: 15 Min | Serves: 4

Ingredient:

- 500g white fish fillets, cut into bite-sized pieces
- 300g potatoes, peeled and diced
- 200g frozen peas
- 1 small onion, finely chopped
- 150ml whole milk
- 50g unsalted butter
- 2 tbsp all-purpose flour
- 1 tsp Dijon mustard
- Salt and pepper to taste
- 1 sheet of puff pastry, thawed
- 1 egg, beaten (for egg wash)

Instruction:

1. In a pot, boil the diced potatoes until tender. Drain and set aside.
2. In a saucepan, melt butter over medium heat. Add chopped onions and cook until softened.
3. Stir in the flour to create a roux. Cook for 1-2 minutes, stirring constantly.
4. Gradually whisk in the milk to form a smooth sauce. Add Dijon mustard, salt, and pepper. Simmer until thickened.
5. Add the cooked potatoes, fish pieces, and frozen peas to the sauce. Gently fold to combine. Allow the mixture to cool slightly.
6. Roll out the puff pastry on a floured surface. Cut circles to fit your air fryer basket or pie molds.
7. Spoon the fish and potato mixture onto half of each pastry circle, leaving a border. Fold the pastry over and seal the edges.
8. Brush the pastry with beaten egg for a golden finish.
9. Place the pies in the air fryer basket. Cook at 180°C for 12-15 minutes or until the pastry is golden and crisp.
10. Carefully remove the fish pies from the air fryer and let them cool for a few minutes before serving.
11. Enjoy these delightful **Fish Pies** with a side of your favorite sauce or a wedge of lemon!

Cottage Pies

Prep: 25 Min | Cook: 18 Min | Serves: 4

Ingredient:

- 500g minced beef
- 1 onion, finely chopped
- 2 carrots, diced
- 2 cloves garlic, minced
- 400g canned chopped tomatoes
- 300ml beef stock
- 2 tbsp tomato paste
- 1 tsp Worcestershire sauce
- 800g potatoes, peeled and chopped
- 50g butter
- Salt and pepper to taste

Instruction:

1. In a pan over medium heat, cook minced beef until browned. Drain excess fat.
2. Add chopped onions, diced carrots, and minced garlic to the beef. Cook until vegetables are softened.
3. Stir in canned tomatoes, tomato paste, Worcestershire sauce, and beef stock. Simmer for 15-20 minutes until the mixture thickens. Season with salt and pepper.
4. Meanwhile, boil the peeled and chopped potatoes until tender. Drain and mash with butter until smooth. Season with salt and pepper.
5. Spoon the beef mixture into individual ramekins or an air fryer-safe dish, leaving space for the mashed potatoes.
6. Top the beef mixture with a layer of mashed potatoes, spreading it evenly.
7. Place the ramekins or dish in the air fryer basket.
8. Cook at 180°C for 15-18 minutes or until the mashed potatoes are golden and the filling is bubbling.
9. Carefully remove the **Cottage Pies** from the air fryer and let them rest for a few minutes.
10. Serve hot, optionally garnished with chopped fresh parsley.

Chapter 01: Pie & Tart

Pumpkin Pies

Prep: 30 Min | Cook: 30 Min | Serves: 8

Ingredient:

- 500g pumpkin, peeled and diced
- 200g shortcrust pastry (store-bought or homemade)
- 150g granulated sugar
- 2 large eggs
- 250ml double cream
- 1 tsp ground cinnamon
- 1/2 tsp ground nutmeg
- 1/2 tsp ground ginger
- 1/4 tsp salt
- 1 tsp vanilla extract
- Whipped cream and ground cinnamon for serving (optional)

Instruction:

1. Steam or boil the diced pumpkin until tender. Mash it into a smooth puree and let it cool.
2. Roll out the shortcrust pastry and line your pie dish, trimming any excess. Prick the base with a fork.
3. In a bowl, beat the eggs and sugar until well combined.
4. Add the pumpkin puree, double cream, ground cinnamon, ground nutmeg, ground ginger, salt, and vanilla extract. Mix until smooth.
5. Pour the pumpkin mixture into the prepared pie crust.
6. Place the pie dish in the air fryer basket.
7. Cook at 180°C for 25-30 minutes or until the filling is set and the pastry is golden brown.
8. Check the pie halfway through cooking; if the edges of the crust are browning too quickly, cover them with foil.
9. Carefully remove the **Pumpkin Pies** from the air fryer and let it cool.
10. Once cooled, refrigerate for a few hours or overnight before serving.
11. Optionally, serve slices with a dollop of whipped cream and a sprinkle of ground cinnamon.

Ratatouille Pies

Prep: 30 Min | Cook: 15 Min | Serves: 4

Ingredient:

- 1 large aubergine (eggplant), diced
- 1 zucchini, diced
- 1 red bell pepper, diced
- 1 yellow bell pepper, diced
- 1 red onion, finely chopped
- 2 cloves garlic, minced
- 400g canned chopped tomatoes
- 2 tbsp tomato paste
- 2 tbsp olive oil
- 1 tsp dried thyme
- Salt and pepper to taste
- 200g puff pastry, thawed
- 1 egg, beaten (for egg wash)

Instruction:

1. In a pan, heat olive oil over medium heat. Sauté the chopped red onion and minced garlic until softened.
2. Add the diced aubergine, zucchini, and bell peppers to the pan. Cook until the vegetables are tender.
3. Stir in the canned chopped tomatoes, tomato paste, dried thyme, salt, and pepper. Simmer for 15-20 minutes until the mixture thickens.
4. Roll out the puff pastry on a floured surface and cut circles to fit your air fryer basket or pie molds.
5. Spoon the ratatouille mixture into each pastry circle, leaving a border.
6. Fold the pastry over the filling, creating a half-moon shape, and press the edges to seal.
7. Brush the pastry with beaten egg for a golden finish.
8. Place the pies in the air fryer basket.
9. Cook at 180°C for 12-15 minutes or until the pastry is golden and crisp.
10. Carefully remove the **Ratatouille Pies** from the air fryer and let them cool for a few minutes before serving.

Chapter 01: Pie & Tart

Chicken Korma Pies

Prep: 20 Min | Cook: 15 Min | Serves: 4

Ingredient:

- 500g boneless, skinless chicken thighs, diced
- 1 large onion, finely chopped
- 2 cloves garlic, minced
- 2 tbsp vegetable oil
- 2 tbsp korma curry paste
- 200ml coconut milk
- 100ml chicken stock
- 50g ground almonds
- 1 tbsp desiccated coconut
- Salt and pepper to taste
- 200g puff pastry, thawed
- 1 egg, beaten (for egg wash)

Instruction:

1. In a pan, heat vegetable oil over medium heat. Sauté the chopped onion and minced garlic until softened.
2. Add the diced chicken thighs to the pan and cook until browned.
3. Stir in the korma curry paste and cook for an additional 2 minutes.
4. Pour in the coconut milk and chicken stock. Add ground almonds and desiccated coconut. Season with salt and pepper. Simmer for 15-20 minutes until the sauce thickens.
5. Roll out the puff pastry on a floured surface and cut circles to fit your air fryer basket or pie molds.
6. Spoon the chicken korma mixture into each pastry circle, leaving a border.
7. Fold the pastry over the filling, creating a half-moon shape, and press the edges to seal.
8. Brush the pastry with beaten egg for a golden finish.
9. Place the pies in the air fryer basket. Cook at 180°C for 12-15 minutes or until the pastry is golden and crisp.
10. Carefully remove the **Chicken Korma Pies** from the air fryer and let them cool for a few minutes before serving.

Instruction:

1. In a bowl, combine pork mince, chopped onion, minced garlic, chopped sage, breadcrumbs, and beaten egg.
2. Season the mixture with salt and pepper. Mix until well combined.
3. Roll out the puff pastry on a floured surface and cut circles to fit your air fryer basket or pie molds.
4. Spoon the pork and sage mixture onto one half of each pastry circle, leaving a border.
5. Fold the pastry over the filling, creating a half-moon shape, and press the edges to seal.
6. Brush the pastry with beaten egg for a golden finish.
7. Place the pies in the air fryer basket.
8. Cook at 180°C for 12-15 minutes or until the pastry is golden and the filling is cooked through.
9. Check the pies halfway through cooking; if the edges of the crust are browning too quickly, cover them with foil.
10. Carefully remove the **Pork and Sage Pies** from the air fryer and let them cool for a few minutes before serving.

Pork and Sage Pies

Prep: 20 Min | Cook: 15 Min | Serves: 4

Ingredient:

- 500g pork mince
- 1 onion, finely chopped
- 2 cloves garlic, minced
- 2 tbsp fresh sage, finely chopped
- 2 tbsp breadcrumbs
- 1 egg
- Salt and pepper to taste
- 200g puff pastry, thawed
- 1 egg, beaten (for egg wash)
- Tomato chutney or brown sauce (optional, for serving)

Chapter 01: Pie & Tart

Caramel Apple Pies

Prep: 25 Min | Cook: 15 Min | Serves: 4

Ingredient:

- 4 medium-sized cooking apples, peeled, cored, and diced
- 50g unsalted butter
- 100g light brown sugar
- 1 tsp ground cinnamon
- 1/2 tsp ground nutmeg
- 1 tbsp cornflour
- 200g puff pastry, thawed
- 1 egg, beaten (for egg wash)
- Caramel sauce for drizzling (store-bought or homemade)
- Vanilla ice cream (optional, for serving)

Instruction:

1. In a pan over medium heat, melt the butter. Add the diced apples, brown sugar, ground cinnamon, and ground nutmeg. Cook until the apples are tender.
2. In a small bowl, mix cornflour with a tablespoon of water to create a slurry. Stir the slurry into the apple mixture to thicken the filling. Remove from heat and let it cool.
3. Roll out the puff pastry on a floured surface and cut circles to fit your air fryer basket or pie molds.
4. Spoon the caramel apple mixture onto one half of each pastry circle, leaving a border.
5. Fold the pastry over the filling, creating a half-moon shape, and press the edges to seal.
6. Brush the pastry with beaten egg for a golden finish.
7. Place the pies in the air fryer basket.
8. Cook at 180°C for 12-15 minutes or until the pastry is golden and the filling is hot.
9. Check the pies halfway through cooking; if the edges of the crust are browning too quickly, cover them with foil.
10. Carefully remove the **Caramel Apple Pies** from the air fryer and let them cool for a few minutes before serving.

Instruction:

1. Crush digestive biscuits in a food processor or by placing them in a sealed bag and using a rolling pin.
2. Mix the crushed biscuits with melted butter until well combined. Press the mixture into the base of individual pie dishes or one larger dish to form the crust.
3. In a heatproof bowl, combine dark chocolate, milk chocolate, and double cream.
4. Melt the chocolates and cream together using a bain-marie or microwave in short bursts. Stir until smooth and let it cool slightly.
5. In a separate bowl, beat the softened butter with icing sugar until creamy. Add vanilla extract and eggs to the butter mixture, beating well after each addition.
6. Gradually pour the melted chocolate mixture into the butter and egg mixture, stirring continuously until smooth.
7. Pour the chocolate silk filling over the biscuit crust in the pie dish(es).
8. Cook at 160°C for 15-18 minutes or until the filling is set but still has a slight wobble.
9. Carefully remove the **Chocolate Silk Pies** from the air fryer and let them cool. Optionally, garnish with chocolate shavings or curls before serving.

Chocolate Silk Pies

Prep: 25 Min | Cook: 18 Min | Serves: 6

Ingredient:

- 200g digestive biscuits
- 100g unsalted butter, melted
- 200g dark chocolate, finely chopped
- 100g milk chocolate, finely chopped
- 150ml double cream
- 50g icing sugar
- 1 tsp vanilla extract
- 3 large eggs
- 50g unsalted butter, softened
- Chocolate shavings or curls for garnish (optional)

Chapter 01: Pie & Tart

Lemon Meringue Pies

Prep: 30 Min | Cook: 12 Min | Serves: 6

Ingredient:

For the Crust:
- 200g digestive biscuits
- 100g unsalted butter, melted

For the Lemon Filling:
- 3 large eggs
- 150g granulated sugar
- Zest of 2 lemons
- Juice of 3 lemons (approximately 150ml)
- 50g unsalted butter

For the Meringue Topping:
- 3 large egg whites
- 150g caster sugar
- 1 tsp cornflour

Instruction:

1. Crush digestive biscuits in a food processor or by placing them in a sealed bag and using a rolling pin.
2. Mix the crushed biscuits with melted butter until well combined. Press the mixture into the base of individual pie dishes or one larger dish to form the crust.
3. In a saucepan, whisk together eggs, sugar, lemon zest, lemon juice, and butter for the lemon filling.
4. Cook the mixture over low heat, stirring constantly until it thickens. This will take about 10-12 minutes. Let it cool slightly.
5. Pour the lemon filling over the biscuit crust in the pie dish(es).
6. In a clean, dry bowl, beat egg whites until soft peaks form. Gradually add caster sugar and cornflour while continuing to beat until stiff and glossy.
7. Spoon the meringue over the lemon filling, spreading it to the edges to seal in the filling completely.
8. Create decorative peaks on the meringue using the back of a spoon.
9. Cook at 160°C for 10-12 minutes or until the meringue is golden brown.
10. Carefully remove the **Lemon Meringue Pies** from the air fryer and let them cool before serving.

Rabbit and Leek Pies

Prep: 30 Min | Cook: 25 Min | Serves: 4

Ingredient:

- 500g rabbit meat, cooked and shredded
- 2 leeks, sliced
- 1 onion, finely chopped
- 2 cloves of garlic, minced
- 250ml chicken or vegetable stock
- 1 tsp dried thyme
- Salt and pepper, to taste
- 600g potatoes, peeled and cubed
- 50g butter
- 50ml milk

Instruction:

1. In a pan, sauté the sliced leeks, chopped onion, and minced garlic until softened.
2. Add the shredded rabbit meat to the pan and stir well.
3. Pour in the chicken or vegetable stock and add the dried thyme, salt, and pepper. Simmer for 10 minutes, allowing the flavors to blend. Remove from heat.
4. While the rabbit and leek mixture is simmering, boil the cubed potatoes in a separate pot until tender. Drain and mash with butter and milk until smooth. Season with salt and pepper.
5. Grease four individual pie dishes that fit in your air fryer.
6. Divide the rabbit and leek mixture evenly among the pie dishes, spreading it out in an even layer.
7. Top each pie dish with a generous layer of mashed potatoes, smoothing it out with a spoon or fork.
8. Place the pies in the air fryer basket, leaving some space between them. Cook the pies in the air fryer for 25 minutes at 180°C or until the potato topping is golden and crispy.
9. Remove the **Rabbit and Leek Pies** from the air fryer and let them cool slightly before serving.

Chapter 01: Pie & Tart

Leek and Potato Pies

Prep: 30 Min | Cook: 15 Min | Serves: 4

Ingredient:

For the Filling:
- 500g potatoes, peeled and diced
- 2 large leeks, washed and sliced
- 1 onion, finely chopped
- 2 cloves garlic, minced
- 200ml vegetable stock
- 150ml double cream
- 2 tbsp butter
- Salt and pepper to taste
- Fresh thyme leaves (optional)

For the Pastry:
- 200g puff pastry, thawed
- 1 egg, beaten (for egg wash)

Instruction:

1. Boil the diced potatoes until tender. Drain and set aside.
2. In a pan, melt butter over medium heat. Add chopped onion, minced garlic, and sliced leeks. Cook until softened.
3. Add the boiled potatoes to the leek mixture. Stir in vegetable stock, double cream, and season with salt and pepper. Simmer until the mixture thickens. Add fresh thyme leaves if desired.
4. Roll out the puff pastry on a floured surface and cut circles to fit your air fryer basket or pie molds.
5. Spoon the leek and potato mixture onto one half of each pastry circle, leaving a border.
6. Fold the pastry over the filling, creating a half-moon shape, and press the edges to seal.
7. Brush the pastry with beaten egg for a golden finish.
8. Place the pies in the air fryer basket.
9. Cook at 180°C for 12-15 minutes or until the pastry is golden and the filling is hot.
10. Carefully remove the **Leek and Potato Pies** from the air fryer and let them cool for a few minutes before serving.

Instruction:

1. In a bowl, combine diced pears, granulated sugar, cornflour, ground ginger, lemon juice, and lemon zest. Toss to coat the pears evenly in the mixture.
2. Roll out the puff pastry on a floured surface and cut circles to fit your air fryer basket or pie molds.
3. Spoon the pear filling onto one half of each pastry circle, leaving a border.
4. Fold the pastry over the filling, creating a half-moon shape, and press the edges to seal.
5. Place the pies in the air fryer basket.
6. Brush the pastry with beaten egg for a golden finish.
7. Cook at 180°C for 12-15 minutes or until the pastry is golden and the pear filling is tender.
8. Check the pies halfway through cooking; if the edges of the crust are browning too quickly, cover them with foil.
9. Carefully remove the **Pear and Ginger Pies** from the air fryer and let them cool for a few minutes before serving.
10. Optionally, serve with a scoop of vanilla ice cream or a dollop of whipped cream.

Pear and Ginger Pies

Prep: 20 Min | Cook: 15 Min | Serves: 4

Ingredient:

For the Filling:
- 4 ripe pears, peeled, cored, and diced
- 50g granulated sugar
- 1 tbsp cornflour
- 1 tsp ground ginger
- 1 tbsp lemon juice
- Zest of 1 lemon

For the Pastry:
- 200g puff pastry, thawed
- 1 egg, beaten (for egg wash)

Chapter 01: Pie & Tart

Thai Green Curry Pies

Prep: 25 Min | Cook: 15 Min | Serves: 4

Ingredient:

For the Filling:
- 300g cooked chicken breast, shredded
- 1 can (400ml) coconut milk
- 2 tbsp Thai green curry paste
- 1 red bell pepper, thinly sliced
- 1 courgette, thinly sliced
- 1 carrot, julienned
- 1 tbsp fish sauce
- 1 tbsp brown sugar
- Fresh coriander leaves for garnish (optional)

For the Pastry:
- 200g puff pastry, thawed
- 1 egg, beaten (for egg wash)

Instruction:

1. In a pan, combine coconut milk and Thai green curry paste. Heat over medium heat until the paste is dissolved and the mixture is well combined.
2. Add shredded chicken, sliced red bell pepper, courgette, and julienned carrot to the pan. Cook until the vegetables are slightly tender.
3. Stir in fish sauce and brown sugar. Simmer for an additional 5 minutes. Remove from heat and let it cool.
4. Roll out the puff pastry on a floured surface and cut circles to fit your air fryer basket or pie molds.
5. Spoon the Thai green curry chicken mixture onto one half of each pastry circle, leaving a border.
6. Fold the pastry over the filling, creating a half-moon shape, and press the edges to seal.
7. Place the pies in the air fryer basket.
8. Brush the pastry with beaten egg for a golden finish.
9. Cook at 180°C for 12-15 minutes or until the pastry is golden and the filling is hot.
10. Carefully remove the **Thai Green Curry Pies** from the air fryer and let them cool for a few minutes before serving.
11. Optionally, garnish with fresh coriander leaves before serving.

Instruction:

1. In a pan, melt butter over medium heat. Add chopped onions and cook until softened.
2. Add thinly sliced potatoes to the pan and cook until they are just tender. Season with salt and pepper.
3. In a separate pan, heat whole milk until warm. Stir in grated cheddar cheese until melted and smooth.
4. Combine the cheese mixture with the cooked potatoes and onions. Let the filling cool.
5. Roll out the puff pastry on a floured surface and cut circles to fit your air fryer basket or pie molds.
6. Spoon the potato and cheese mixture onto one half of each pastry circle, leaving a border.
7. Fold the pastry over the filling, creating a half-moon shape, and press the edges to seal.
8. Place the pies in the air fryer basket.
9. Brush the pastry with beaten egg for a golden finish.
10. Cook at 180°C for 12-15 minutes or until the pastry is golden and the filling is hot.
11. Carefully remove the **Potato and Cheese Pies** from the air fryer and let them cool for a few minutes before serving.

Potato and Cheese Pies

Prep: 30 Min | Cook: 15 Min | Serves: 4

Ingredient:

For the Filling:
- 500g potatoes, peeled and thinly sliced
- 1 onion, finely chopped
- 150g grated cheddar cheese
- 150ml whole milk
- 1 tbsp butter
- Salt and pepper to taste
- Fresh chives for garnish (optional)

For the Pastry:
- 200g puff pastry, thawed
- 1 egg, beaten (for egg wash)

Chicken and Pesto Pies

Prep: 30 Min | Cook: 15 Min | Serves: 4

Ingredient:

For the Filling:
- 500g chicken breast, diced
- 2 tbsp pesto sauce
- 1 onion, finely chopped
- 2 cloves garlic, minced
- 200ml double cream
- 50g grated Parmesan cheese
- Salt and pepper to taste
- Fresh basil leaves for garnish (optional)

For the Pastry:
- 200g puff pastry, thawed
- 1 egg, beaten (for egg wash)

Instruction:

1. In a pan, sauté chopped onions and minced garlic until softened.
2. Add diced chicken to the pan and cook until browned.
3. Stir in pesto sauce, double cream, and grated Parmesan cheese. Season with salt and pepper. Simmer until the mixture thickens. Let it cool.
4. Roll out the puff pastry on a floured surface and cut circles to fit your air fryer basket or pie molds.
5. Spoon the chicken and pesto mixture onto one half of each pastry circle, leaving a border.
6. Fold the pastry over the filling, creating a half-moon shape, and press the edges to seal.
7. Place the pies in the air fryer basket.
8. Brush the pastry with beaten egg for a golden finish.
9. Cook at 180°C for 12-15 minutes or until the pastry is golden and the filling is hot.
10. Carefully remove the **Chicken and Pesto Pies** from the air fryer and let them cool for a few minutes before serving.
11. Optionally, garnish with fresh basil leaves before serving.

Instruction:

1. In a pan, heat olive oil over medium heat. Add chopped onions and sauté until softened.
2. Add pork sausage meat to the pan, breaking it up with a spatula. Cook until browned.
3. Stir in diced apples, wholegrain mustard, salt, and pepper. Cook for an additional 3-5 minutes until apples are tender. Let it cool.
4. Roll out the puff pastry on a floured surface and cut circles to fit your air fryer basket or pie molds.
5. Spoon the sausage and apple mixture onto one half of each pastry circle, leaving a border.
6. Fold the pastry over the filling, creating a half-moon shape, and press the edges to seal.
7. Place the pies in the air fryer basket.
8. Brush the pastry with beaten egg for a golden finish.
9. Cook at 180°C for 12-15 minutes or until the pastry is golden and the filling is hot.
10. Carefully remove the **Sausage and Apple Pies** from the air fryer and let them cool for a few minutes before serving.
11. Optionally, garnish with chopped fresh parsley before serving.

Sausage and Apple Pies

Prep: 25 Min | Cook: 15 Min | Serves: 4

Ingredient:

For the Filling:
- 400g pork sausages, casings removed
- 2 apples, peeled, cored, and diced
- 1 onion, finely chopped
- 2 tbsp olive oil
- 1 tbsp wholegrain mustard
- Salt and pepper to taste
- Fresh parsley, chopped, for garnish (optional)

For the Pastry:
- 200g puff pastry, thawed
- 1 egg, beaten (for egg wash)

Turkey and Stuffing Pies

Prep: 30 Min | Cook: 25 Min | Serves: 4

Ingredient:

- 300g cooked turkey, shredded
- 200g stuffing, cooked and crumbled
- 1 tablespoon butter
- 1 small onion, finely chopped
- 1 garlic clove, minced
- 200ml turkey or chicken gravy
- 320g ready-made puff pastry, thawed
- 1 egg, beaten (for egg wash)
- Salt and pepper to taste

Instruction:

1. Sauté onion and garlic in butter. Add shredded turkey and crumbled stuffing. Pour in gravy, season with salt and pepper. Let mixture cool slightly.
2. Roll out the puff pastry on a lightly floured surface to about 0.5cm thickness. Cut out 8 circles for the pie bases and 4 slightly larger circles for the pie tops.
3. Line 4 individual pie dishes with the smaller pastry circles, pressing the edges to seal.
4. Divide the turkey and stuffing mixture equally among the pie dishes.
5. Place the larger pastry circles on top of each pie dish, pressing the edges to seal. Make a small slit on the top of each pie to allow steam to escape.
6. Brush the pastry with beaten egg.
7. Place the assembled pies in the air fryer basket, ensuring they are not touching each other.
8. Cook in the air fryer at 180°C for 25 minutes or until the pastry is golden and cooked through.
9. Once cooked, remove the **Turkey and Stuffing Pies** from the air fryer and let them cool slightly before serving.

Guinness and Onion Pies

Prep: 30 Min | Cook: 15 Min | Serves: 4

Ingredient:

For the Filling:
- 2 large onions, thinly sliced
- 400g beef stewing meat, diced
- 2 tbsp plain flour
- 330ml Guinness or stout
- 200ml beef stock
- 2 tbsp tomato paste
- 1 tsp Worcestershire sauce
- Salt and pepper to taste
- 2 tbsp vegetable oil

For the Pastry:
- 200g puff pastry, thawed
- 1 egg, beaten (for egg wash)

Instruction:

1. In a bowl, toss the diced beef in flour until evenly coated.
2. In a pan, heat vegetable oil over medium heat. Brown the floured beef until sealed on all sides.
3. Add thinly sliced onions to the pan and cook until softened.
4. Pour in Guinness, beef stock, tomato paste, and Worcestershire sauce. Stir well and bring to a simmer. Season with salt and pepper.
5. Simmer for 1.5 to 2 hours or until the beef is tender and the sauce has thickened. Let it cool.
6. Roll out the puff pastry on a floured surface and cut circles to fit your air fryer basket or pie molds.
7. Spoon the Guinness and onion mixture onto one half of each pastry circle, leaving a border.
8. Fold the pastry over the filling, creating a half-moon shape, and press the edges to seal.
9. Place the pies in the air fryer basket.
10. Brush the pastry with beaten egg for a golden finish.
11. Cook at 180°C for 12-15 minutes or until the pastry is golden and the filling is hot.
12. Enjoy the **Guinness and Onion Pies**!

Beef and Horseradish Pies

Prep: 30 Min | Cook: 15 Min | Serves: 4

Ingredient:

For the Filling:
- 500g beef steak, diced
- 2 tbsp plain flour
- 1 onion, finely chopped
- 2 cloves garlic, minced
- 200ml beef stock
- 2 tbsp horseradish sauce
- 1 tbsp Worcestershire sauce
- Salt and pepper to taste
- 2 tbsp vegetable oil

For the Pastry:
- 200g puff pastry, thawed
- 1 egg, beaten (for egg wash)

Instruction:

1. In a bowl, toss the diced beef in flour until evenly coated.
2. In a pan, heat vegetable oil over medium heat. Brown the floured beef until sealed on all sides.
3. Add chopped onions and minced garlic to the pan. Cook until softened.
4. Pour in beef stock, horseradish sauce, and Worcestershire sauce. Stir well and bring to a simmer. Season with salt and pepper.
5. Simmer for 1.5 to 2 hours or until the beef is tender and the sauce has thickened. Let it cool.
6. Roll out the puff pastry on a floured surface and cut circles to fit your air fryer basket or pie molds.
7. Spoon the beef and horseradish mixture onto one half of each pastry circle, leaving a border.
8. Fold the pastry over the filling, creating a half-moon shape, and press the edges to seal.
9. Place the pies in the air fryer basket. Brush the pastry with beaten egg for a golden finish. Cook at 180°C for 12-15 minutes or until the pastry is golden and the filling is hot. Enjoy the **Beef and Horseradish Pies!**

Instruction:

1. Cook chicken until browned. Remove and set aside. Sauté mushrooms, onion, and garlic until softened. Add butter and flour to form a roux. Gradually pour in chicken stock while stirring.
2. Return chicken to the pan. Pour in milk, season with salt and pepper. Simmer for 5 minutes. Remove from heat and cool.
3. Roll out the puff pastry on a floured surface to a thickness of about 0.5cm. Cut out 4 circles of pastry, slightly larger than the individual pie dishes you'll be using.
4. Grease pie dishes. Divide cooled filling among them. Place pastry circles on top, pressing edges to seal. Brush pastry tops with beaten egg.
5. Using a sharp knife, make a few slits on the pastry to allow steam to escape during baking.
6. Place the pies in the air fryer basket, leaving some space between them.
7. Cook the pies in the air fryer 180°C for 25 minutes or until the pastry is golden brown and flaky.
8. Remove the **Chicken and Mushroom Pies** from the air fryer and let them cool slightly before serving.

Chicken and Mushroom Pies

Prep: 30 Min | Cook: 25 Min | Serves: 4

Ingredient:

- 500g chicken breast, diced
- 200g mushrooms, sliced
- 1 onion, finely chopped
- 2 cloves of garlic, minced
- 250ml chicken stock
- 2 tbsp flour
- 2 tbsp butter
- 250ml milk
- Salt and pepper, to taste
- 600g puff pastry
- 1 egg, beaten (for egg wash)

Chapter 01: Pie & Tart

Mocha Tarts

Prep: 30 Min | Cook: 18 Min | Serves: 6

Ingredient:

For the Tart Shells:
- 200g plain flour
- 100g unsalted butter, cold and diced
- 1 tbsp cocoa powder
- 2 tbsp icing sugar
- 1-2 tbsp cold water

For the Mocha Filling:
- 150g dark chocolate, chopped
- 150ml double cream
- 1 tbsp instant coffee granules
- 1 tbsp golden syrup
- 2 large eggs, beaten

Instruction:

1. In a food processor, combine plain flour, cold diced butter, cocoa powder, and icing sugar. Pulse until the mixture resembles breadcrumbs.
2. Gradually add cold water, one tablespoon at a time, and pulse until the dough comes together.
3. Gather the dough into a ball, wrap it in cling film, and refrigerate for at least 30 minutes.
4. Roll out the chilled dough on a floured surface and use it to line tart tins.
5. Prick the base of each tart with a fork and place them in the air fryer basket.
6. In a saucepan, heat double cream until it just starts to simmer. Remove from heat and add chopped dark chocolate, instant coffee granules, and golden syrup. Stir until smooth.
7. Allow the chocolate mixture to cool slightly, then whisk in beaten eggs until well combined.
8. Pour the mocha filling into the tart shells.
9. Cook the tarts in the air fryer at 160°C for 15-18 minutes or until the filling is set.
10. Carefully remove the **Mocha Tarts** from the air fryer and let them cool before serving.

Instruction:

1. In a food processor, combine plain flour, cold diced butter, and salt. Pulse until the mixture resembles breadcrumbs.
2. Gradually add cold water, one tablespoon at a time, and pulse until the dough comes together.
3. Gather the dough into a ball, wrap it in cling film, and refrigerate for at least 30 minutes.
4. Roll out the chilled dough on a floured surface and use it to line tart tins.
5. Prick the base of each tart with a fork and place them in the air fryer basket.
6. Cook the tart shells in the air fryer at 180°C for 10-12 minutes or until they are golden and crisp. Allow them to cool.
7. Arrange halved cherry tomatoes and sliced fresh mozzarella in the tart shells.
8. Drizzle extra virgin olive oil over the tomato and mozzarella filling.
9. Season with salt and black pepper to taste.
10. Place the tarts back in the air fryer and cook for an additional 5 minutes at 180°C or until the mozzarella is slightly melted.
11. Remove the **Caprese Tarts** from the air fryer, top with fresh basil leaves, and drizzle with balsamic glaze before serving.

Caprese Tarts

Prep: 30 Min | Cook: 12 Min | Serves: 4

Ingredient:

For the Tart Shells:
- 200g plain flour
- 100g unsalted butter, cold and diced
- 1/2 tsp salt
- 2-3 tbsp cold water

For the Filling:
- 200g cherry tomatoes, halved
- 150g fresh mozzarella, sliced
- Fresh basil leaves
- 2 tbsp extra virgin olive oil
- Balsamic glaze for drizzling
- Salt and black pepper to taste

Chapter 01: Pie & Tart

Key Lime Tarts

Prep: 30 Min | Cook: 22 Min | Serves: 6

Ingredient:

For the Tart Shells:
- 200g digestive biscuits
- 75g unsalted butter, melted

For the Key Lime Filling:
- Zest of 4 limes
- 150ml lime juice (about 6-8 limes)
- 4 large eggs
- 200g granulated sugar
- 150g unsalted butter, melted
- 1 tbsp cornflour

For Garnish:
- Whipped cream
- Lime slices or zest

Instruction:

1. Crush digestive biscuits into fine crumbs using a food processor or by placing them in a sealed bag and using a rolling pin.
2. Combine the biscuit crumbs with melted butter, mixing until the crumbs are evenly coated.
3. Press the biscuit mixture into tart tins to form the crust. Place the tart tins in the air fryer basket.
4. Cook the tart shells in the air fryer at 160°C for 5-7 minutes until set. Allow them to cool.
5. In a bowl, whisk together lime zest, lime juice, eggs, granulated sugar, melted butter, and cornflour until well combined.
6. Pour the lime mixture into the cooled tart shells.
7. Cook the tarts in the air fryer at 160°C for 12-15 minutes or until the filling is set.
8. Allow the Key Lime Tarts to cool completely before refrigerating for at least 2 hours to set.
9. Once chilled, remove the tarts from the fridge and garnish with whipped cream and lime slices or zest.
10. Serve the **Key Lime Tarts** chilled.

Instruction:

1. Roll out the shortcrust pastry on a floured surface and cut circles to fit your tart molds.
2. Line the tart molds with the pastry circles, pressing them gently into the corners. Trim any excess pastry.
3. In a bowl, combine blackberries, caster sugar, cornflour, lemon zest, and lemon juice. Gently mix to coat the blackberries evenly.
4. Spoon the blackberry mixture into the pastry-lined tart molds.
5. Fold the edges of the pastry over the blackberry filling, creating a rustic, free-form tart.
6. Brush the pastry edges with beaten egg for a golden finish.
7. Place the tart molds in the air fryer. Cook at 180°C for 15 minutes or until the pastry is golden and the blackberry filling is bubbly.
8. Once cooled, dust the Blackberry Tarts with icing sugar.
9. Serve the tarts on their own or with a dollop of whipped cream or a scoop of vanilla ice cream.
10. Enjoy the burst of British flavors in these delightful **Blackberry Tarts!**

Blackberry Tarts

Prep: 20 Min | Cook: 15 Min | Serves: 6

Ingredient:

- 250g shortcrust pastry
- 200g fresh blackberries
- 75g caster sugar
- 1 tbsp cornflour
- Zest of 1 lemon
- 1 tbsp lemon juice
- 1 egg, beaten (for egg wash)
- Icing sugar for dusting

Maple Pecan Tarts

Prep: 30 Min | Cook: 30 Min | Serves: 6

Ingredient:

For the Tart Shells:
- 200g plain flour
- 100g unsalted butter, cold and diced
- 1 tbsp icing sugar
- 2-3 tbsp cold water

For the Filling:
- 150g pecan halves
- 2 large eggs
- 150g maple syrup
- 75g light brown sugar
- 50g unsalted butter, melted
- 1 tsp vanilla extract
- Pinch of salt

Instruction:

1. In a food processor, combine plain flour, cold diced butter, and icing sugar. Pulse until the mixture resembles breadcrumbs.
2. Gradually add cold water, one tablespoon at a time, and pulse until the dough comes together.
3. Gather the dough into a ball, wrap it in cling film, and refrigerate for at least 30 minutes.
4. Roll out the chilled dough on a floured surface and use it to line tart tins.
5. Prick the base of each tart with a fork and place them in the air fryer basket.
6. Cook the tart shells in the air fryer at 180°C for 10-12 minutes or until they are golden and crisp. Allow them to cool.
7. In a bowl, whisk together eggs, maple syrup, light brown sugar, melted butter, vanilla extract, and a pinch of salt.
8. Place pecan halves in the cooled tart shells.
9. Pour the maple and egg mixture over the pecans.
10. Cook the tarts in the air fryer at 160°C for 15-18 minutes or until the filling is set.
11. Allow the **Maple Pecan Tarts** to cool before serving.

Instruction:

1. In a food processor, combine plain flour, cold diced butter, and salt. Pulse until the mixture resembles breadcrumbs.
2. Gradually add cold water, one tablespoon at a time, and pulse until the dough comes together.
3. Gather the dough into a ball, wrap it in cling film, and refrigerate for at least 30 minutes. Roll out the chilled dough on a floured surface and use it to line tart tins.
4. Prick the base of each tart with a fork and place them in the air fryer basket.
5. Cook the tart shells in the air fryer at 180°C for 10-12 minutes or until they are golden and crisp. Allow them to cool.
6. In a pan, heat olive oil and sauté chopped onions and minced garlic until softened.
7. Add diced aubergine, courgette, red and yellow bell peppers to the pan. Cook until the vegetables are tender.
8. Stir in chopped tomatoes, dried oregano, dried thyme, salt, and black pepper. Simmer until the mixture thickens.
9. Spoon the ratatouille mixture into the cooled tart shells.
10. Place the tarts back in the air fryer and cook for an additional 5-7 minutes at 180°C or until the filling is heated through.
11. Serve the **Ratatouille Tarts** chilled.

Ratatouille Tarts

Prep: 30 Min | Cook: 20 Min | Serves: 4

Ingredient:

- 200g plain flour
- 100g unsalted butter, cold and diced
- 1/2 tsp salt
- 2-3 tbsp cold water
- 1 small aubergine, diced
- 1 small courgette, diced
- 1 red bell pepper, diced
- 1 yellow bell pepper, diced
- 1 red onion, finely chopped
- 2 cloves garlic, minced
- 400g tin chopped tomatoes
- 1 tsp dried oregano
- 1 tsp dried thyme

Chapter 01: Pie & Tart

Blood Orange Tarts

Prep: 30 Min | Cook: 22 Min | Serves: 6

Ingredient:

For the Tart Shells:
- 200g plain flour
- 100g unsalted butter, cold and diced
- 1 tbsp icing sugar
- 2-3 tbsp cold water

For the Blood Orange Curd:
- Zest of 3 blood oranges
- 200ml blood orange juice (about 4-5 blood oranges)
- 150g granulated sugar
- 3 large eggs
- 100g unsalted butter, diced

For Garnish:
- Icing sugar for dusting

Instruction:

1. In a food processor, combine plain flour, cold diced butter, and icing sugar. Pulse until the mixture resembles breadcrumbs.
2. Gradually add cold water, one tablespoon at a time, and pulse until the dough comes together.
3. Gather the dough into a ball, wrap it in cling film, and refrigerate for at least 30 minutes.
4. Roll out the chilled dough on a floured surface and use it to line tart tins.
5. Prick the base of each tart with a fork and place them in the air fryer basket.
6. Cook the tart shells in the air fryer at 180°C for 10-12 minutes or until they are golden and crisp. Allow them to cool.
7. In a saucepan, whisk together blood orange zest, blood orange juice, granulated sugar, and eggs over medium heat.
8. Add diced butter and continue whisking until the mixture thickens into a curd-like consistency. Remove from heat and let it cool.
9. Spoon the blood orange curd into the cooled tart shells.
10. Dust the **Blood Orange Tarts** with icing sugar before serving.

Black Forest Tarts

Prep: 30 Min | Cook: 12 Min | Serves: 6

Ingredient:

For the Tart Shells:
- 200g plain flour
- 100g unsalted butter, cold and diced
- 1 tbsp icing sugar
- 2-3 tbsp cold water

For the Black Forest Filling:
- 150g dark chocolate, finely chopped
- 150ml double cream
- 2 tbsp cherry jam or preserves
- 200g canned pitted cherries, drained
- Whipped cream for topping
- Chocolate shavings for garnish (optional)

Instruction:

1. In a food processor, combine plain flour, cold diced butter, and icing sugar. Pulse until the mixture resembles breadcrumbs.
2. Gradually add cold water, one tablespoon at a time, and pulse until the dough comes together.
3. Gather the dough into a ball, wrap it in cling film, and refrigerate for at least 30 minutes.
4. Roll out the chilled dough on a floured surface and use it to line tart tins.
5. Prick the base of each tart with a fork and place them in the air fryer basket.
6. Cook the tart shells in the air fryer at 180°C for 10-12 minutes or until they are golden and crisp. Allow them to cool.
7. In a saucepan, heat double cream until it just starts to simmer. Remove from heat and add finely chopped dark chocolate. Stir until smooth.
8. Spread a layer of cherry jam or preserves onto the cooled tart shells. Pour the chocolate mixture over the jam layer.
9. Top the tarts with canned pitted cherries and a dollop of whipped cream. Serve the **Black Forest Tarts**.

Cherry Almond Tarts

Prep: 30 Min | Cook: 12 Min | Serves: 6

Ingredient:

- 200g plain flour
- 100g unsalted butter, cold and diced
- 1 tbsp icing sugar
- 2-3 tbsp cold water
- 100g ground almonds
- 75g unsalted butter, softened
- 75g caster sugar
- 2 large eggs
- 1 tsp almond extract
- 200g fresh cherries, pitted and halved
- 2 tbsp cherry jam or preserves
- Flaked almonds for garnish

Instruction:

1. In a food processor, combine plain flour, cold diced butter, and icing sugar. Pulse until the mixture resembles breadcrumbs.
2. Gradually add cold water, one tablespoon at a time, and pulse until the dough comes together.
3. Gather the dough into a ball, wrap it in cling film, and refrigerate for at least 30 minutes.
4. Roll out the chilled dough on a floured surface and use it to line tart tins.
5. Prick the base of each tart with a fork and place them in the air fryer basket.
6. Cook the tart shells in the air fryer at 180°C for 10-12 minutes or until they are golden and crisp. Allow them to cool.
7. In a bowl, beat together ground almonds, softened butter, caster sugar, eggs, and almond extract until well combined.
8. Spread the almond filling into the cooled tart shells.
9. Arrange pitted and halved cherries on top of the almond filling.
10. Warm cherry jam or preserves and brush it over the cherry topping for a glossy finish.
11. Sprinkle flaked almonds on top and serve the **Cherry Almond Tarts**.

Instruction:

1. In a food processor, combine plain flour, cold diced butter, and icing sugar. Pulse until the mixture resembles breadcrumbs.
2. Gradually add cold water, one tablespoon at a time, and pulse until the dough comes together.
3. Gather the dough into a ball, wrap it in cling film, and refrigerate for at least 30 minutes.
4. Roll out the chilled dough on a floured surface and use it to line tart tins.
5. Prick the base of each tart with a fork and place them in the air fryer basket.
6. Cook the tart shells in the air fryer at 180°C for 10-12 minutes or until they are golden and crisp. Allow them to cool.
7. In a bowl, whip together double cream, icing sugar, and rose water until soft peaks form.
8. Spoon the rose-infused cream into the cooled tart shells.
9. Arrange fresh raspberries on top of the cream.
10. Warm raspberry jam or preserves and brush it over the raspberry topping for a shiny finish.
11. Optionally, garnish with edible rose petals before serving.
12. Serve the **Raspberry Rose Tarts**.

Raspberry Rose Tarts

Prep: 30 Min | Cook: 12 Min | Serves: 6

Ingredient:

For the Tart Shells:
- 200g plain flour
- 100g unsalted butter, cold and diced
- 1 tbsp icing sugar
- 2-3 tbsp cold water

For the Rose-Infused Cream:
- 200ml double cream
- 2 tbsp icing sugar
- 1 tsp rose water

For the Raspberry Topping:
- 200g fresh raspberries
- 2 tbsp raspberry jam or preserves
- Edible rose petals for garnish (optional)

Cinnamon Apple Tarts

Prep: 20 Min | Cook: 15 Min | Serves: 4 tarts

Ingredient:

For the Filling:
- 2 large Bramley apples, peeled, cored, and diced
- 50g caster sugar
- 1 tsp ground cinnamon
- 1 tbsp water

For the Pastry:
- 1 sheet ready-rolled shortcrust pastry (about 320g)
- 1 egg, lightly beaten for glazing
- A little flour, for dusting

To Serve (optional):
- Icing sugar, for dusting
- Whipped cream or vanilla ice cream

Instruction:

1. In a saucepan over medium heat, combine the diced apples, caster sugar, cinnamon, and water. Cook for about 5-7 minutes until the apples are soft but not mushy. Set aside to cool.
2. Dust a clean surface with a little flour and unroll the pastry sheet. Cut into 4 equal squares.
3. Spoon the cooled apple mixture onto the center of each pastry square, leaving a border around the edges.
4. Fold the edges of the pastry over the apple mixture, pinching at the corners to create a rustic tart shape. Lightly brush the pastry with beaten egg to glaze.
5. Place the tarts in the air fryer basket, ensuring they are not touching. Set the air fryer to 180°C and cook for 15 minutes, or until the pastry is golden and crisp.
6. Let the tarts cool for a few minutes after cooking. Dust with icing sugar before serving. Serve **Cinnamon Apple Tarts** warm with a dollop of whipped cream or a scoop of vanilla ice cream, if desired.

Instruction:

1. In a food processor, combine plain flour, cold diced butter, and salt. Pulse until the mixture resembles breadcrumbs.
2. Gradually add cold water, one tablespoon at a time, and pulse until the dough comes together.
3. Gather the dough into a ball, wrap it in cling film, and refrigerate for at least 30 minutes.
4. Roll out the chilled dough on a floured surface and use it to line tart tins.
5. Prick the base of each tart with a fork and place them in the air fryer basket.
6. Cook the tart shells in the air fryer at 180°C for 10-12 minutes or until they are golden and crisp. Allow them to cool.
7. In a bowl, mix crumbled feta, sliced black olives, sliced green olives, chopped fresh parsley, chopped fresh oregano, extra virgin olive oil, and black pepper.
8. Spoon the feta and olive mixture into the cooled tart shells.
9. Place the tarts back in the air fryer and cook for an additional 5-7 minutes at 180°C or until the filling is heated through.
10. Garnish with fresh parsley or oregano leaves before serving.
11. Serve the **Feta and Olive Tarts**.

Feta and Olive Tarts

Prep: 30 Min | Cook: 20 Min | Serves: 6

Ingredient:

- 200g plain flour
- 100g unsalted butter, cold and diced
- 1/2 tsp salt
- 2-3 tbsp cold water
- 150g feta cheese, crumbled
- 50g pitted black olives, sliced
- 50g pitted green olives, sliced
- 1 tbsp fresh parsley, chopped
- 1 tbsp fresh oregano, chopped
- 2 tbsp extra virgin olive oil
- Black pepper, to taste
- Fresh parsley or oregano leaves (optional)

Chapter 01: Pie & Tart

Cherry Bakewell Tarts

Prep: 30 Min | Cook: 12 Min | Serves: 6

Ingredient:

- 200g plain flour
- 100g unsalted butter, cold and diced
- 1 tbsp icing sugar
- 2-3 tbsp cold water
- 100g unsalted butter, softened
- 100g caster sugar
- 2 large eggs
- 1 tsp almond extract
- 100g ground almonds
- 150g cherry jam or preserves
- 100g glace cherries, halved
- 100g icing sugar
- 2 tbsp water

Instruction:

1. In a food processor, combine plain flour, cold diced butter, and icing sugar. Pulse until the mixture resembles breadcrumbs.
2. Gradually add cold water, one tablespoon at a time, and pulse until the dough comes together.
3. Gather the dough into a ball, wrap it in cling film, and refrigerate for at least 30 minutes.
4. Roll out the chilled dough on a floured surface and use it to line tart tins. Prick the base of each tart with a fork and place them in the air fryer basket.
5. Cook the tart shells in the air fryer at 180°C for 10-12 minutes or until they are golden and crisp. Allow them to cool.
6. In a bowl, beat together softened butter, caster sugar, eggs, almond extract, and ground almonds to make the frangipane filling.
7. Spoon the frangipane filling into the cooled tart shells.
8. In a saucepan, heat cherry jam or preserves until it's slightly melted. Spoon it over the frangipane filling.
9. Top each tart with halved glace cherries.
10. In a separate bowl, mix icing sugar, water, and almond extract to make the icing. Drizzle it over the tarts.
11. Serve the **Cherry Bakewell Tarts**.

Instruction:

1. In a large bowl, mix the flour and caster sugar. Rub in the butter with your fingertips until the mixture resembles fine breadcrumbs.
2. Gradually add cold water, mixing until the dough comes together. Form into a ball, wrap in clingfilm, and chill in the fridge for 15 minutes.
3. In a bowl, toss the sliced plums with brown sugar, ground ginger, and cinnamon (if using) until well coated.
4. Roll out the pastry on a lightly floured surface to about 3mm thickness. Cut out rounds to fit your tart tins or molds that are air fryer-safe.
5. Press the pastry into each tin, trimming any excess. Prick the bottom with a fork.
6. Divide the plum mixture among the pastry cases.
7. Preheat the air fryer for a few minutes at 180°C if your model requires preheating.
8. Place the tart tins in the air fryer basket. Bake at 180°C for 12-15 minutes, or until the pastry is golden and the plums are tender.
9. Allow the **tarts** to cool slightly before removing from the tins.
10. Dust with icing sugar before serving. Offer with whipped cream or a scoop of vanilla ice cream on the side for added indulgence.

Plum and Ginger Tarts

Prep: 20 Min | Cook: 15 Min | Serves: 4 tarts

Ingredient:

For the Pastry:
- 200g plain flour, plus extra for dusting
- 100g cold unsalted butter, cubed
- 2-3 tbsp cold water
- 1 tbsp caster sugar

For the Filling:
- 4 plums, pitted and sliced
- 2 tbsp brown sugar
- 1 tsp ground ginger
- 1/2 tsp cinnamon (optional)

To Serve (optional):
- Icing sugar for dusting
- Whipped cream or vanilla ice cream

Chapter 01: Pie & Tart

Chocolate Orange Tarts

Prep: 30 Min | Cook: 12 Min | Serves: 6

Ingredient:

- 200g plain flour
- 100g unsalted butter, cold and diced
- 1 tbsp icing sugar
- 2-3 tbsp cold water
- 200g dark chocolate, finely chopped
- 200ml double cream
- Zest of 1 orange
- 2 tbsp orange marmalade
- Orange segments or curls (optional)

Instruction:

1. In a food processor, combine plain flour, cold diced butter, and icing sugar. Pulse until the mixture resembles breadcrumbs.
2. Gradually add cold water, one tablespoon at a time, and pulse until the dough comes together.
3. Gather the dough into a ball, wrap it in cling film, and refrigerate for at least 30 minutes.
4. Roll out the chilled dough on a floured surface and use it to line tart tins.
5. Prick the base of each tart with a fork and place them in the air fryer basket.
6. Cook the tart shells in the air fryer at 180°C for 10-12 minutes or until they are golden and crisp. Allow them to cool.
7. In a heatproof bowl, place finely chopped dark chocolate.
8. In a saucepan, heat double cream until it just begins to simmer. Pour the hot cream over the chocolate and let it sit for a minute. Stir until smooth.
9. Stir in the orange zest and orange marmalade into the chocolate mixture. Spoon the chocolate orange ganache into the cooled tart shells.
10. Optionally, garnish with orange segments or curls before serving. Serve the **Chocolate Orange Tarts**.

Instruction:

1. In a food processor, combine plain flour, cold diced butter, and icing sugar. Pulse until the mixture resembles breadcrumbs.
2. Gradually add cold water, one tablespoon at a time, and pulse until the dough comes together.
3. Gather the dough into a ball, wrap it in cling film, and refrigerate for at least 30 minutes.
4. Roll out the chilled dough on a floured surface and use it to line tart tins.
5. Prick the base of each tart with a fork and place them in the air fryer basket.
6. Cook the tart shells in the air fryer at 180°C for 10-12 minutes or until they are golden and crisp. Allow them to cool.
7. In a heatproof bowl, place finely chopped dark chocolate.
8. In a saucepan, heat double cream and caster sugar until it just begins to simmer. Pour the hot cream over the chocolate and let it sit for a minute. Stir until smooth.
9. Stir in vanilla extract into the chocolate mixture.
10. Allow the chocolate mixture to cool slightly, then spoon it into the cooled tart shells.
11. Refrigerate the tarts for at least 2 hours or until the chocolate mousse is set. Garnish with grated chocolate or chocolate curls and fresh berries if desired. Serve the **Chocolate Mousse Tarts**.

Chocolate Mousse Tarts

Prep: 30 Min | Cook: 12 Min | Serves: 6

Ingredient:

- 200g plain flour
- 100g unsalted butter, cold and diced
- 1 tbsp icing sugar
- 2-3 tbsp cold water
- 200g dark chocolate, finely chopped
- 300ml double cream
- 50g caster sugar
- 1 tsp vanilla extract
- Grated chocolate or chocolate curls
- Fresh berries (optional)

Chapter 01: Pie & Tart

Lemon Blackberry Tarts

Prep: 25 Min | Cook: 15 Min | Serves: 6

Ingredient:

- 250g shortcrust pastry
- 150g blackberries
- Zest of 2 lemons
- 125g caster sugar
- 2 medium eggs
- 150ml double cream
- 1 tbsp plain flour
- 1 tsp vanilla extract
- Icing sugar for dusting
- Fresh mint leaves for garnish (optional)

Instruction:

1. Roll out the shortcrust pastry on a floured surface and cut circles to fit your tart molds. Line the tart molds with the pastry circles, pressing them gently into the corners. Trim any excess pastry.
2. In a bowl, mix blackberries and lemon zest. Spoon the mixture into the pastry-lined tart molds.
3. In a separate bowl, whisk together caster sugar, eggs, double cream, plain flour, and vanilla extract until well combined.
4. Pour the egg mixture over the blackberries, ensuring even distribution.
5. Place the tart molds in the air fryer. Cook at 180°C for 15 minutes or until the pastry is golden and the lemon-blackberry filling is set.
6. Once cooled, dust the Lemon Blackberry Tarts with icing sugar.
7. Optional: Garnish with fresh mint leaves for a burst of color and flavor.
8. Serve these refreshing tarts at room temperature, embracing the delightful British taste.
9. Optional: Pair with a dollop of whipped cream or a scoop of vanilla ice cream for added indulgence.
10. Enjoy your **Lemon Blackberry Tarts** with a hint of British sophistication!

Instruction:

1. In a food processor, combine plain flour, cold diced butter, and icing sugar. Pulse until the mixture resembles breadcrumbs.
2. Gradually add cold water, one tablespoon at a time, and pulse until the dough comes together.
3. Gather the dough into a ball, wrap it in cling film, and refrigerate for at least 30 minutes. Roll out the chilled dough on a floured surface and use it to line tart tins. Prick the base of each tart with a fork and place them in the air fryer basket.
4. Cook the tart shells in the air fryer at 180°C for 10-12 minutes or until they are golden and crisp. Allow them to cool.
5. Dissolve instant coffee granules in hot water to make a strong coffee.
6. In a bowl, beat together softened cream cheese and icing sugar until smooth. Gradually add the strong coffee to the cream cheese mixture, stirring continuously.
7. In a separate bowl, whip the double cream until soft peaks form. Fold the whipped cream into the coffee and cream cheese mixture.
8. Stir in finely chopped walnuts. Spoon the **Coffee and Walnut Tarts** filling into the cooled tart shells. Garnish with additional chopped walnuts and chocolate shavings if desired.

Coffee and Walnut Tarts

Prep: 30 Min | Cook: 12 Min | Serves: 6

Ingredient:

- 200g plain flour
- 100g unsalted butter, cold and diced
- 2-3 tbsp cold water
- 2 tbsp instant coffee granules
- 2 tbsp hot water
- 200g cream cheese, softened
- 75g icing sugar
- 150ml double cream
- 50g walnuts, finely chopped
- Chopped walnuts
- Chocolate shavings (optional)

Chapter 01: Pie & Tart

Orange and Cardamom Tarts

Prep: 30 Min | Cook: 30 Min | Serves: 6

Ingredient:

- 200g plain flour
- 100g unsalted butter, cold and diced
- 1 tbsp icing sugar
- 2-3 tbsp cold water
- Zest of 2 oranges
- Juice of 2 oranges
- 150g caster sugar
- 3 large eggs
- 150ml double cream
- 1 tsp ground cardamom
- Orange zest twists or slices
- Icing sugar for dusting

Instruction:

1. In a food processor, combine plain flour, cold diced butter, and icing sugar. Pulse until the mixture resembles breadcrumbs.
2. Gradually add cold water, one tablespoon at a time, and pulse until the dough comes together.
3. Gather the dough into a ball, wrap it in cling film, and refrigerate for at least 30 minutes.
4. Roll out the chilled dough on a floured surface and use it to line tart tins.
5. Prick the base of each tart with a fork and place them in the air fryer basket.
6. Cook the tart shells in the air fryer at 180°C for 10-12 minutes or until they are golden and crisp. Allow them to cool.
7. In a bowl, whisk together orange zest, orange juice, caster sugar, eggs, double cream, and ground cardamom.
8. Pour the orange and cardamom mixture into the cooled tart shells.
9. Cook the tarts in the air fryer at 160°C for 15-18 minutes or until the filling is set.
10. Allow the tarts to cool before garnishing with orange zest twists or slices and a dusting of icing sugar.
11. Serve the **Orange and Cardamom Tarts**.

Blueberry Cheesecake Tarts

Prep: 30 Min | Cook: 30 Min | Serves: 6

Ingredient:

- 200g plain flour
- 100g unsalted butter, cold and diced
- 1 tbsp icing sugar
- 2-3 tbsp cold water
- 200g cream cheese, softened
- 75g caster sugar
- 1 large egg
- 1 tsp vanilla extract
- 150ml double cream
- 150g fresh blueberries
- 2 tbsp blueberry jam or preserves
- Fresh mint leaves (optional)

Instruction:

1. In a food processor, combine plain flour, cold diced butter, and icing sugar. Pulse until the mixture resembles breadcrumbs.
2. Gradually add cold water, one tablespoon at a time, and pulse until the dough comes together.
3. Gather the dough into a ball, wrap it in cling film, and refrigerate for at least 30 minutes.
4. Roll out the chilled dough on a floured surface and use it to line tart tins.
5. Prick the base of each tart with a fork and place them in the air fryer basket.
6. Cook the tart shells in the air fryer at 180°C for 10-12 minutes or until they are golden and crisp. Allow them to cool.
7. In a bowl, beat together softened cream cheese, caster sugar, egg, vanilla extract, and double cream until smooth.
8. Spoon the cheesecake filling into the cooled tart shells.
9. Cook the tarts in the air fryer at 160°C for 15-18 minutes or until the cheesecake is set.
10. In a small saucepan, warm blueberry jam or preserves. Gently stir in fresh blueberries until they are coated.
11. Spoon the blueberry mixture over the cheesecake filling. Optionally, garnish with fresh mint leaves. Serve the **Blueberry Cheesecake Tarts**.

Chapter 01: Pie & Tart

Mocha Cake

Prep: 15 Min | Cook: 30 Min | Serves: 8 slices

Ingredient:

- 200g self-raising flour
- 200g unsalted butter, softened
- 200g golden caster sugar
- 4 large eggs
- 2 tablespoons cocoa powder
- 2 tablespoons instant coffee granules dissolved in 2 tablespoons hot water
- 1 teaspoon vanilla extract
- 100g dark chocolate, melted
- 150ml whole milk
- 1 teaspoon baking powder
- Pinch of salt

Instruction:

1. In a large mixing bowl, cream together the softened butter and golden caster sugar until light and fluffy.
2. Add the eggs one at a time, beating well after each addition.
3. Sift in the self-raising flour, cocoa powder, and baking powder. Add a pinch of salt, then gently fold the dry ingredients into the wet ingredients.
4. Stir in the dissolved coffee, melted dark chocolate, and vanilla extract. Gradually add the milk while continuing to mix until you achieve a smooth and well-combined batter.
5. Grease the air fryer cake pan with a little butter or use parchment paper to prevent sticking.
6. Pour the cake batter into the prepared pan, spreading it evenly.
7. Place the cake pan in the air fryer basket.
8. Set the air fryer to 160°C and cook for 25-30 minutes, or until a toothpick inserted into the center comes out clean.
9. Once cooked, carefully remove the cake from the air fryer and allow it to cool in the pan for 10 minutes before transferring it to a wire rack to cool completely.
10. Once cooled, you can dust the cake with cocoa powder or icing sugar for decoration. Enjoy your delicious **Mocha Cake** with a rich coffee and chocolate flavor

---

Instruction:

1. In a bowl, mix together the light brown sugar, cinnamon, and nutmeg.
2. Add the cold cubed butter and flour. Rub together with your fingertips until the mixture resembles coarse breadcrumbs. Set aside half of this mixture for the filling and the other half for the topping.
3. In another large bowl, whisk together the plain flour, caster sugar, salt, baking powder, and ground cinnamon (if using).
4. In a separate bowl, mix the milk, egg, melted butter, and vanilla extract.
5. Combine the wet ingredients with the dry ingredients, stirring until just blended. Do not overmix.
6. If your air fryer requires it, lightly grease the air fryer basket or use an air fryer-safe baking pan that fits inside the basket.
7. Pour half of the batter into the prepared pan. Sprinkle the reserved streusel filling evenly over the batter.
8. Top with the remaining batter, smoothing it gently. Finish by sprinkling the remaining streusel topping over the batter.
9. Set the air fryer to 160°C and bake the cake for 20-25 minutes, or until a toothpick inserted into the center comes out clean. The exact cooking time may vary depending on the air fryer model.
10. Allow the **Coffee Cake** to cool slightly before serving. This cake is best enjoyed warm or at room temperature, alongside your favorite coffee.

Coffee Cake

Prep: 20 Min | Cook: 25 Min | Serves: 8 slices

Ingredient:

- 200g plain flour
- 150g caster sugar
- 1/2 tsp salt
- 2 tsp baking powder
- 1/3 tsp ground cinnamon (optional, for the batter)
- 100ml milk
- 1 large egg
- 4 tbsp unsalted butter, melted
- 1 tsp vanilla extract

For the Streusel Topping and Filling:
- 100g light brown sugar
- 2 tsp ground cinnamon
- 1/2 tsp ground nutmeg (optional)
- 4 tbsp unsalted butter, cold and cubed
- 75g plain flour

Chapter 02: Cakes

Coconut Cake

Prep: 15 Min | Cook: 30 Min | Serves: 8

Ingredient:

- 200g self-raising flour
- 200g unsalted butter, softened
- 200g caster sugar
- 4 large eggs
- 100g desiccated coconut
- 1 teaspoon baking powder
- 1 teaspoon vanilla extract
- 150ml coconut milk
- 100g icing sugar
- 2 tablespoons coconut milk
- 50g desiccated coconut (for decoration)

Instruction:

1. In a large mixing bowl, cream together the softened butter and caster sugar until light and fluffy.
2. Add the eggs one at a time, beating well after each addition.
3. Sift in the self-raising flour and baking powder. Gently fold the dry ingredients into the wet ingredients.
4. Stir in the desiccated coconut and vanilla extract.
5. Gradually add the coconut milk while continuing to mix until you achieve a smooth and well-combined batter.
6. Grease the air fryer cake pan with a little butter or use parchment paper to prevent sticking.
7. Pour the cake batter into the prepared pan, spreading it evenly.
8. Place the cake pan in the air fryer basket.
9. Set the air fryer to 160°C and cook for 25-30 minutes, or until a toothpick inserted into the center comes out clean.
10. While the cake is cooking, prepare the coconut glaze by mixing icing sugar with coconut milk until smooth.
11. Once the cake is cooked, drizzle the coconut glaze over the top and sprinkle desiccated coconut for decoration.
12. Delight in this **Coconut Cake** with a tropical twist, perfectly suited to British tastes!

Instruction:

1. In a large mixing bowl, cream together the softened butter and golden caster sugar until light and fluffy.
2. Add the eggs one at a time, beating well after each addition.
3. Sift in the self-raising flour, cocoa powder, and baking powder. Gently fold the dry ingredients into the wet ingredients.
4. Stir in the chopped salted peanuts, chocolate chips, and vanilla extract.
5. Grease the air fryer cake pan with a little butter or use parchment paper to prevent sticking.
6. Pour half of the cake batter into the prepared pan, then drizzle half of the caramel sauce on top. Repeat with the remaining batter and caramel sauce.
7. Place the cake pan in the air fryer basket.
8. Set the air fryer to 160°C and cook for 25-30 minutes, or until a toothpick inserted into the center comes out clean.
9. While the cake is cooking, prepare the chocolate ganache by melting dark chocolate with double cream and golden syrup. Mix until smooth.
10. Once the **Snickers Cake** is cooked, drizzle the chocolate ganache over the top.
11. Allow the cake to cool for 10 minutes in the pan before transferring it to a wire rack to cool completely.

Snickers Cake

Prep: 20 Min | Cook: 30 Min | Serves: 8

Ingredient:

- 200g self-raising flour
- 200g unsalted butter, softened
- 200g golden caster sugar
- 4 large eggs
- 2 tablespoons cocoa powder
- 100g salted peanuts, chopped
- 1 teaspoon baking powder
- 1 teaspoon vanilla extract
- 150g chocolate chips
- 150g caramel sauce
- 100g dark chocolate, chopped
- 100ml double cream
- 2 tablespoons golden syrup

Chapter 02: Cakes

Pecan Pie Cake

Prep: 20 Min | Cook: 30 Min | Serves: 8

Ingredient:

- 200g self-raising flour
- 200g unsalted butter, softened
- 200g light brown sugar
- 4 large eggs
- 100g chopped pecans
- 1 teaspoon baking powder
- 1 teaspoon vanilla extract
- 50g golden syrup
- Pinch of salt
- 100g pecan halves

Instruction:

1. In a large mixing bowl, cream together the softened butter and light brown sugar until light and fluffy.
2. Add the eggs one at a time, beating well after each addition.
3. Sift in the self-raising flour, baking powder, and a pinch of salt. Gently fold the dry ingredients into the wet ingredients.
4. Stir in the chopped pecans and vanilla extract.
5. Grease the air fryer cake pan with a little butter or use parchment paper to prevent sticking.
6. Pour half of the cake batter into the prepared pan, then prepare the pecan pie filling.
7. For the pecan pie filling, heat golden syrup, light brown sugar, and butter in a saucepan until melted and smooth. Remove from heat, stir in vanilla extract, and fold in pecan halves.
8. Spoon the pecan pie filling over the first layer of cake batter, then top with the remaining batter.
9. Place the cake pan in the air fryer basket.
10. Set the air fryer to 160°C and cook for 25-30 minutes, or until a toothpick inserted into the center comes out clean.
11. Once cooked, allow the cake to cool for 10 minutes in the pan before transferring it to a wire rack to cool completely.
12. Savor the rich flavors of **Pecan Pie Cake.**

Red Velvet Cake

Prep: 15 Min | Cook: 30 Min | Serves: 8

Ingredient:

- 200g self-raising flour
- 200g caster sugar
- 200g unsalted butter, softened
- 4 large eggs
- 2 tablespoons cocoa powder
- 1 teaspoon baking powder
- 1 teaspoon vanilla extract
- 150ml buttermilk
- Red food coloring (about 2-3 tablespoons)
- 200g cream cheese, softened
- 100g icing sugar

Instruction:

1. In a large mixing bowl, cream together the softened butter and caster sugar until light and fluffy.
2. Add the eggs one at a time, beating well after each addition.
3. Sift in the self-raising flour, cocoa powder, and baking powder. Gently fold the dry ingredients into the wet ingredients.
4. Stir in the buttermilk, vanilla extract, and red food coloring. Mix until you achieve a smooth and well-combined batter.
5. Grease the air fryer cake pan with a little butter or use parchment paper to prevent sticking.
6. Pour the cake batter into the prepared pan, spreading it evenly.
7. Place the cake pan in the air fryer basket.
8. Set the air fryer to 160°C and cook for 25-30 minutes, or until a toothpick inserted into the center comes out clean.
9. While the cake is cooking, prepare the cream cheese frosting by beating together cream cheese, icing sugar, butter, and vanilla extract until smooth.
10. Once the cake is cooked, allow it to cool for 10 minutes in the pan before transferring it to a wire rack to cool completely.
11. Once the cake is completely cool, spread the cream cheese frosting over the top.
12. Enjoy this classic **Red Velvet Cake** with luscious cream cheese frosting, perfect for British taste buds!

Chapter 02: Cakes

Hummingbird Cake

Prep: 15 Min | Cook: 30 Min | Serves: 8

Ingredient:

- 200g self-raising flour
- 200g ripe bananas, mashed
- 200g canned crushed pineapple, drained
- 200g light brown sugar
- 100g chopped pecans
- 2 large eggs
- 150ml vegetable oil
- 1 teaspoon ground cinnamon
- 1 teaspoon vanilla extract
- 1/2 teaspoon baking soda
- A pinch of salt

Instruction:

1. In a large mixing bowl, combine mashed bananas, drained crushed pineapple, and chopped pecans.
2. In a separate bowl, whisk together the vegetable oil, eggs, and vanilla extract.
3. Add the oil mixture to the banana mixture and mix well.
4. In another bowl, sift together the self-raising flour, light brown sugar, ground cinnamon, baking soda, and a pinch of salt.
5. Gradually add the dry ingredients to the wet ingredients, stirring until just combined.
6. Grease the air fryer cake pan with a little oil or use parchment paper to prevent sticking.
7. Pour the cake batter into the prepared pan, spreading it evenly.
8. Place the cake pan in the air fryer basket.
9. Set the air fryer to 160°C and cook for 25-30 minutes, or until a toothpick inserted into the center comes out clean.
10. Allow the cake to cool in the pan for 10 minutes before transferring it to a wire rack to cool completely.
11. Once cooled, you can optionally dust the cake with icing sugar or top it with cream cheese frosting for added sweetness.
12. Indulge in this delightful **Hummingbird Cake** with tropical flavors, tailored to British tastes!

Key Lime Pie Cake

Prep: 20 Min | Cook: 15 Min | Serves: 6

Ingredient:

- 200g digestive biscuits
- 100g unsalted butter, melted
- 400g cream cheese, softened
- 150g caster sugar
- Zest and juice of 4 limes
- 4 large eggs
- 200ml double cream
- 1 tsp vanilla extract
- Icing sugar for dusting
- Lime slices for garnish (optional)

Instruction:

1. Crush the digestive biscuits until fine. Mix with melted butter until the crumbs are coated.
2. Press the biscuit mixture into the base of the air fryer basket, creating a firm crust.
3. In a large bowl, beat together cream cheese and caster sugar until smooth.
4. Add the zest and juice of the limes to the cream cheese mixture, mixing well.
5. Beat in the eggs one at a time until fully incorporated.
6. Pour in the double cream and add vanilla extract. Mix until the batter is creamy and smooth.
7. Pour the cream cheese mixture over the biscuit base in the air fryer basket.
8. Place the air fryer basket in the air fryer. Cook at 160°C for 15 minutes or until the edges are set, and the centre has a slight wobble.
9. Once cooked, remove the basket from the air fryer and let the Key Lime Pie Cake cool for a few minutes.
10. Dust the top with icing sugar.
11. Optional: Garnish with lime slices for a decorative touch.
12. Refrigerate the **Key Lime Pie Cake** for at least 2 hours before serving.

Chapter 02: Cakes

Pumpkin Spice Cake

Prep: 15 Min | Cook: 30 Min | Serves: 8

Ingredient:

- 200g self-raising flour
- 200g canned pumpkin puree
- 150g light brown sugar
- 2 large eggs
- 100ml vegetable oil
- 1 teaspoon ground cinnamon
- 1/2 teaspoon ground nutmeg
- 1/2 teaspoon ground ginger
- 1/4 teaspoon ground cloves
- 1 teaspoon baking powder
- A pinch of salt

Instruction:

1. In a large mixing bowl, whisk together the pumpkin puree, light brown sugar, eggs, and vegetable oil until well combined.
2. In a separate bowl, sift together the self-raising flour, ground cinnamon, ground nutmeg, ground ginger, ground cloves, baking powder, and a pinch of salt.
3. Gradually add the dry ingredients to the wet ingredients, stirring until just combined.
4. Grease the air fryer cake pan with a little oil or use parchment paper to prevent sticking.
5. Pour the cake batter into the prepared pan, spreading it evenly.
6. Place the cake pan in the air fryer basket.
7. Set the air fryer to 160°C and cook for 25-30 minutes, or until a toothpick inserted into the center comes out clean.
8. Allow the cake to cool in the pan for 10 minutes before transferring it to a wire rack to cool completely.
9. Once cooled, you can optionally dust the cake with icing sugar or frost it with cream cheese frosting for added sweetness.
10. Slice and serve the **Pumpkin Spice Cake**.

Vanilla Pound Cake

Prep: 15 Min | Cook: 30 Min | Serves: 8

Ingredient:

- 225g unsalted butter, softened
- 225g caster sugar
- 4 large eggs
- 225g self-raising flour
- 1 teaspoon vanilla extract
- 2 tablespoons whole milk

Instruction:

1. In a large mixing bowl, cream together the softened butter and caster sugar until light and fluffy.
2. Add the eggs one at a time, beating well after each addition.
3. Sift in the self-raising flour and fold it gently into the mixture.
4. Stir in the vanilla extract to the batter.
5. Add the whole milk and mix until you achieve a smooth and well-combined batter.
6. Grease the air fryer cake pan with a little butter or use parchment paper to prevent sticking.
7. Pour the cake batter into the prepared pan, spreading it evenly.
8. Place the cake pan in the air fryer basket.
9. Set the air fryer to 160°C and cook for 25-30 minutes, or until a toothpick inserted into the center comes out clean.
10. Allow the cake to cool in the pan for 10 minutes before transferring it to a wire rack to cool completely.
11. Once cooled, you can dust the cake with icing sugar for decoration or serve it with a dollop of whipped cream.
12. Indulge in the classic simplicity of **Vanilla Pound Cake**, perfectly suited to British taste buds!

Chapter 02: Cakes

Earl Grey Tea Cake

Prep: 20 Min | Cook: 30 Min | Serves: 8

Ingredient:

- 200g self-raising flour
- 150g unsalted butter, softened
- 150g caster sugar
- 3 large eggs
- 2 Earl Grey tea bags
- 3 tablespoons milk
- 1 teaspoon baking powder
- 1 teaspoon vanilla extract
- Zest of 1 lemon
- Pinch of salt

Instruction:

1. In a small saucepan, heat the milk until warm but not boiling. Add the contents of the Earl Grey tea bags to the milk, stir, and let it steep for 5 minutes. Strain out the tea leaves and set the infused milk aside to cool.
2. In a large mixing bowl, cream together the softened butter and caster sugar until light and fluffy.
3. Add the eggs one at a time, beating well after each addition.
4. Sift in the self-raising flour, baking powder, and a pinch of salt. Gently fold the dry ingredients into the wet ingredients.
5. Stir in the Earl Grey infused milk, vanilla extract, and lemon zest. Mix until you achieve a smooth and well-combined batter.
6. Grease the air fryer cake pan with a little butter or use parchment paper to prevent sticking.
7. Pour the cake batter into the prepared pan, spreading it evenly.
8. Place the cake pan in the air fryer basket.
9. Set the air fryer to 160°C and cook for 25-30 minutes, or until a toothpick inserted into the center comes out clean.
10. Allow the cake to cool in the pan for 10 minutes before transferring it to a wire rack to cool completely.
11. Once cooled, you can dust the **Earl Grey Tea Cake** with icing sugar or serve it with a side of whipped cream.

Instruction:

1. In a large bowl, sift together the flour, baking powder, bicarbonate of soda, cinnamon, nutmeg, cloves, ginger, and salt.
2. In another bowl, whisk together the caster sugar, vegetable oil, eggs, pumpkin puree, and vanilla extract until well combined.
3. Gradually add the wet ingredients to the dry ingredients, stirring until just combined. Be careful not to overmix.
4. Grease and line an air fryer-safe cake pan that fits inside your air fryer basket.
5. Pour the batter into the prepared pan, smoothing the top with a spatula.
6. Set the air fryer to 160°C and bake for 25-30 minutes, or until a skewer inserted into the centre of the cake comes out clean. Depending on the size of your air fryer, you may need to adjust the cooking time.
7. Allow the cake to cool in the pan for about 10 minutes, then transfer it to a wire rack to cool completely.
8. Beat together the softened butter and cream cheese until smooth.
9. Gradually add the icing sugar and vanilla extract, beating until creamy and spreadable.
10. Once the cake is completely cool, spread the cream cheese frosting over the top.
11. Slice and serve the **pumpkin cake**.

Pumpkin Cake

Prep: 15 Min | Cook: 30 Min | Serves: 8

Ingredient:

- 200g plain flour
- 2 tsp baking powder
- 1/2 tsp bicarbonate of soda
- 1 tsp ground cinnamon
- 1/2 tsp ground nutmeg
- 1/4 tsp ground cloves
- 1/4 tsp ground ginger
- A pinch of salt
- 200g caster sugar
- 100ml vegetable oil
- 2 large eggs
- 200g pumpkin puree (canned or homemade)
- 1 tsp vanilla extract

For the Cream Cheese Frosting (optional):
- 50g unsalted butter, softened
- 100g cream cheese, at room temperature
- 200g icing sugar, sifted
- 1/2 tsp vanilla extract

Chapter 02: Cakes

Pistachio Rose Cake

Prep: 20 Min | Cook: 15 Min | Serves: 8

Ingredient:

- 200g unsalted butter, softened
- 200g caster sugar
- 4 large eggs
- 200g self-raising flour
- 100g shelled pistachios, finely ground
- 1 tsp baking powder
- 2 tbsp rose water
- 150g icing sugar
- 2 tbsp milk
- Pistachio nuts and dried rose petals for garnish (optional)

Instruction:

1. In a large mixing bowl, cream together softened butter and caster sugar until light and fluffy.
2. Add the eggs one at a time, beating well after each addition.
3. In a separate bowl, sift together self-raising flour and baking powder.
4. Gradually fold the flour mixture into the wet ingredients until well combined.
5. Stir in finely ground pistachios and rose water.
6. Grease and line the base of the air fryer basket with parchment paper.
7. Pour the cake batter into the prepared basket, spreading it evenly.
8. Place the air fryer basket in the air fryer. Cook at 160°C for 15 minutes or until a skewer inserted into the centre comes out clean.
9. Once cooked, remove the basket from the air fryer and let the cake cool for a few minutes.
10. Mix together icing sugar and milk to create the icing. Drizzle over the warm cake.
11. Optional: Garnish with whole pistachio nuts and dried rose petals for a visually appealing touch. Enjoy elegant **Pistachio Rose Cake**!

Instruction:

1. In a large mixing bowl, cream together the softened butter and caster sugar until light and fluffy.
2. Add the eggs one at a time, beating well after each addition.
3. Sift in the self-raising flour, ground cinnamon, baking powder, and a pinch of salt. Gently fold the dry ingredients into the wet ingredients.
4. Stir in the diced apples and vanilla extract.
5. If using, add the raisins and mix well.
6. Gradually add the milk while continuing to mix until you achieve a smooth and well-combined batter.
7. Grease the air fryer cake pan with a little butter or use parchment paper to prevent sticking.
8. Pour the cake batter into the prepared pan, spreading it evenly.
9. Place the cake pan in the air fryer basket.
10. Set the air fryer to 160°C and cook for 25-30 minutes, or until a toothpick inserted into the center comes out clean.
11. Allow the cake to cool in the pan for 10 minutes before transferring it to a wire rack to cool completely.
12. Enjoy the delightful combination of apples and cinnamon with this easy-to-make **Apple Cinnamon Cake**, perfect for British taste buds!

Apple Cinnamon Cake

Prep: 15 Min | Cook: 30 Min | Serves: 8

Ingredient:

- 200g self-raising flour
- 150g unsalted butter, softened
- 150g caster sugar
- 2 large eggs
- 2 apples, peeled, cored, and diced
- 1 teaspoon ground cinnamon
- 1 teaspoon baking powder
- 1 teaspoon vanilla extract
- 50g raisins (optional)
- 3 tablespoons milk
- A pinch of salt

Chapter 02: Cakes

Chocolate Mint Cake

Prep: 20 Min | Cook: 30 Min | Serves: 6

Ingredient:

- 200g self-raising flour
- 150g unsalted butter, softened
- 150g caster sugar
- 2 large eggs
- 2 tablespoons cocoa powder
- 1 teaspoon baking powder
- 1 teaspoon peppermint extract
- Green food coloring (optional)
- 3 tablespoons milk
- 150g dark chocolate, melted
- 200g icing sugar

Instruction:

1. In a large mixing bowl, cream together the softened butter and caster sugar until light and fluffy.
2. Add the eggs one at a time, beating well after each addition.
3. Sift in the self-raising flour, cocoa powder, and baking powder. Gently fold the dry ingredients into the wet ingredients.
4. Stir in the melted dark chocolate, peppermint extract, and green food coloring if desired.
5. Gradually add the milk while continuing to mix until you achieve a smooth and well-combined batter.
6. Grease the air fryer cake pan with a little butter or use parchment paper to prevent sticking.
7. Pour the cake batter into the prepared pan, spreading it evenly.
8. Place the cake pan in the air fryer basket.
9. Set the air fryer to 160°C and cook for 25-30 minutes, or until a toothpick inserted into the center comes out clean.
10. While the cake is cooking, prepare the mint icing by beating together icing sugar, softened butter, peppermint extract, and green food coloring until smooth.
11. Once the **Chocolate Mint Cake** is cooked, allow it to cool in the pan for 10 minutes before transferring it to a wire rack to cool completely. Once cooled, spread the mint icing over the top.

Instruction:

1. In a large mixing bowl, cream together the softened butter and caster sugar until light and fluffy.
2. Add the eggs one at a time, beating well after each addition.
3. Sift in the self-raising flour, baking powder, and a pinch of salt. Gently fold the dry ingredients into the wet ingredients.
4. Stir in the mashed bananas and vanilla extract.
5. In a small microwave-safe bowl, heat the Nutella for a few seconds until it becomes easier to work with. Swirl the Nutella into the batter, leaving some streaks for a marbled effect.
6. Add the chopped hazelnuts to the batter and mix until evenly distributed.
7. Grease the air fryer cake pan with a little butter or use parchment paper to prevent sticking.
8. Pour the cake batter into the prepared pan, spreading it evenly.
9. Place the cake pan in the air fryer basket.
10. Set the air fryer to 160°C and cook for 25-30 minutes, or until a toothpick inserted into the center comes out clean.
11. Allow the cake to cool in the pan for 10 minutes before transferring it to a wire rack to cool completely.
12. Enjoy the delightful fusion of bananas and Nutella with this **Banana Nutella Cake**, tailored to British taste buds!

Banana Nutella Cake

Prep: 15 Min | Cook: 30 Min | Serves: 8

Ingredient:

- 200g self-raising flour
- 150g unsalted butter, softened
- 150g caster sugar
- 2 large ripe bananas, mashed
- 2 large eggs
- 2 tablespoons Nutella
- 1 teaspoon vanilla extract
- 1 teaspoon baking powder
- 50g chopped hazelnuts
- A pinch of salt

Chapter 02: Cakes

Rhubarb Crumble Cake

Prep: 20 Min | Cook: 15 Min | Serves: 6

Ingredient:

For the Cake:
- 200g unsalted butter, softened
- 200g caster sugar
- 4 large eggs
- 200g self-raising flour
- 1 tsp baking powder
- 1 tsp vanilla extract
- 200g fresh rhubarb, chopped

For the Crumble Topping:
- 75g plain flour
- 50g unsalted butter, cold and diced
- 50g demerara sugar

Instruction:

1. In a large mixing bowl, cream together softened butter and caster sugar until light and fluffy.
2. Add the eggs one at a time, beating well after each addition.
3. In a separate bowl, sift together self-raising flour and baking powder.
4. Gradually fold the flour mixture into the wet ingredients until well combined.
5. Stir in vanilla extract and fold in the chopped rhubarb.
6. Grease and line the base of the air fryer basket with parchment paper.
7. Pour the cake batter into the prepared basket, spreading it evenly.
8. In a small bowl, combine plain flour, cold diced butter, and demerara sugar to create the crumble topping.
9. Sprinkle the crumble mixture evenly over the cake batter.
10. Place the air fryer basket in the air fryer. Cook at 160°C for 15 minutes or until a skewer inserted into the centre comes out clean.
11. Once cooked, remove the basket from the air fryer and let the cake cool for a few minutes. Serve slices of this delightful **Rhubarb Crumble Cake**!

Victoria Sponge Cake

Prep: 15 Min | Cook: 25 Min | Serves: 8

Ingredient:

- 200g self-raising flour
- 200g unsalted butter, softened
- 200g caster sugar
- 4 large eggs
- 1 teaspoon baking powder
- 1 teaspoon vanilla extract
- Strawberry jam
- 200ml double cream
- Icing sugar (for dusting)

Instruction:

1. In a large mixing bowl, cream together the softened butter and caster sugar until light and fluffy.
2. Add the eggs one at a time, beating well after each addition.
3. Sift in the self-raising flour and baking powder. Gently fold the dry ingredients into the wet ingredients.
4. Stir in the vanilla extract.
5. Grease the air fryer cake pan with a little butter or use parchment paper to prevent sticking.
6. Pour the cake batter into the prepared pan, spreading it evenly.
7. Place the cake pan in the air fryer basket.
8. Set the air fryer to 160°C and cook for 20-25 minutes, or until a toothpick inserted into the center comes out clean.
9. Allow the cake to cool in the pan for 10 minutes before transferring it to a wire rack to cool completely.
10. Once cooled, spread strawberry jam on one half of the cake.
11. Whip the double cream until it forms soft peaks and spread it on the other half. Sandwich the two halves together, and dust the top with icing sugar.
12. Indulge in the classic elegance of **Victoria Sponge Cake**, a timeless British treat made effortlessly in the air fryer!

Chapter 02: Cakes

Blueberry Lemon Cake

Prep: 20 Min | Cook: 30 Min | Serves: 8

Ingredient:

- 200g self-raising flour
- 150g unsalted butter, softened
- 150g caster sugar
- 3 large eggs
- Zest of 2 lemons
- 2 tablespoons lemon juice
- 150g fresh blueberries
- 1 teaspoon baking powder
- 3 tablespoons milk
- Icing sugar (for dusting)

Instruction:

1. In a large mixing bowl, cream together the softened butter and caster sugar until light and fluffy.
2. Add the eggs one at a time, beating well after each addition.
3. Sift in the self-raising flour and baking powder. Gently fold the dry ingredients into the wet ingredients.
4. Stir in the lemon zest and lemon juice.
5. Gradually add the milk while continuing to mix until you achieve a smooth and well-combined batter.
6. Grease the air fryer cake pan with a little butter or use parchment paper to prevent sticking.
7. Fold in the fresh blueberries into the batter.
8. Pour the cake batter into the prepared pan, spreading it evenly.
9. Place the cake pan in the air fryer basket.
10. Set the air fryer to 160°C and cook for 25-30 minutes, or until a toothpick inserted into the center comes out clean.
11. Allow the cake to cool in the pan for 10 minutes before transferring it to a wire rack to cool completely.
12. Delight in the refreshing combination of blueberries and lemon with this easy-to-make **Blueberry Lemon Cake**, perfect for British taste buds!

Instruction:

1. Line a baking tray with parchment paper. Heat the caster sugar and water in a pan over medium heat until the sugar dissolves and turns amber. Add the hazelnuts, stir quickly, and spread onto the tray to harden. Once set, crush into coarse pieces.
2. In a bowl, cream together the butter and caster sugar until light and fluffy. Beat in the eggs one at a time, then fold in the self-raising flour, baking powder, and ground hazelnuts. Stir in the milk to reach a dropping consistency.
3. Divide the batter between two greased and lined air fryer-safe cake pans that fit your air fryer model.
4. Cook each layer at 160°C for about 20 minutes or until a skewer inserted comes out clean. Allow to cool before removing from the pans.
5. Beat the softened butter until creamy, then gradually add the icing sugar, milk, and vanilla extract until smooth and spreadable.
6. Once the cakes are cool, spread a layer of buttercream on one cake layer, sprinkle with some of the hazelnut praline pieces, then top with the second cake layer. Spread the remaining buttercream over the top and sides of the cake. Decorate with the remaining praline pieces and whole hazelnuts.
7. Allow the **Hazelnut Praline Cake** to set slightly, then slice and serve.

Hazelnut Praline Cake

Prep: 45 Min | Cook: 20 Min | Serves: 8

Ingredient:

For the Hazelnut Praline:
- 100g caster sugar
- 50ml water
- 100g hazelnuts, toasted and skinned

For the Cake:
- 200g unsalted butter, softened
- 200g caster sugar
- 4 eggs
- 200g self-raising flour
- 1 tsp baking powder
- 100g ground hazelnuts
- 2 tbsp milk

For the Filling/Decoration:
- Hazelnut praline pieces
- Whole hazelnuts, toasted and skinned (optional)

For the Buttercream:
- 150g unsalted butter, softened
- 300g icing sugar, sifted
- 2-3 tbsp milk
- 1 tsp vanilla extract

Chapter 02: Cakes

Raspberry Cake

Prep: 15 Min | Cook: 30 Min | Serves: 8

Ingredient:

- 200g self-raising flour
- 175g caster sugar
- 1/2 tsp baking powder
- A pinch of salt
- 4 eggs
- 175g unsalted butter, melted
- 1 tsp vanilla extract
- 200g fresh raspberries (reserve some for topping)
- Icing sugar, for dusting (optional)

Instruction:

1. In a large mixing bowl, sift together the self-raising flour, caster sugar, baking powder, and a pinch of salt.
2. In a separate bowl, whisk the eggs, then mix in the melted butter and vanilla extract until well combined.
3. Gradually incorporate the wet ingredients into the dry ingredients, mixing until just combined to form a smooth batter.
4. Gently fold in most of the raspberries, reserving some for the topping.
5. Grease and line an air fryer-safe cake pan that fits inside your air fryer basket.
6. Pour the cake batter into the prepared pan, smoothing the top with a spatula.
7. Gently press the reserved raspberries into the top of the batter.
8. Set the air fryer to 160°C and bake for 25-30 minutes, or until a skewer inserted into the centre comes out clean. The cooking time may vary depending on the air fryer model.
9. Allow the **Raspberry Cake** to cool in the pan for a few minutes before transferring it to a wire rack to cool completely.
10. Once cooled, dust with icing sugar if desired before serving.

Instruction:

1. In a bowl, mix together the plain flour, ground hazelnuts, baking powder, and salt. Set aside.
2. In another large bowl, whisk the egg yolks with half of the caster sugar (100g) until pale and creamy.
3. Gradually mix in the vegetable oil, milk, and vanilla extract into the yolk mixture.
4. Fold the dry ingredients into the wet mixture until just combined.
5. In a clean, dry bowl, beat the egg whites until soft peaks form. Gradually add the remaining 100g of caster sugar and continue beating until stiff peaks form.
6. Gently fold the egg whites into the cake batter, being careful not to deflate the mixture.
7. Grease and line an air fryer-safe cake pan that fits inside your air fryer basket.
8. Pour the batter into the prepared pan, smoothing the top with a spatula.
9. Set the air fryer to 160°C and bake for 25-30 minutes, or until a skewer inserted into the centre of the cake comes out clean. The exact cooking time may vary depending on your air fryer model.
10. While the cake is cooling, mix the icing sugar with enough milk to achieve a thick but pourable consistency.
11. Once the cake has cooled, drizzle the glaze over the top and sprinkle with chopped hazelnuts for garnish.
12. Allow the glaze to set before slicing the cake. Serve **Hazelnut Cake** as is or with a dollop of whipped cream or a scoop of ice cream for an extra indulgent treat.

Hazelnut Cake

Prep: 20 Min | Cook: 30 Min | Serves: 8

Ingredient:

- 150g plain flour
- 100g ground hazelnuts
- 1 tsp baking powder
- 1/4 tsp salt
- 4 eggs, separated
- 200g caster sugar, divided
- 100ml vegetable oil
- 100ml milk
- 1 tsp vanilla extract

For the Glaze (optional):
- 100g icing sugar
- 1-2 tbsp milk or as needed
- Chopped hazelnuts for garnish

Chapter 02: Cakes

Raspberry Ripple Cake

Prep: 15 Min | Cook: 30 Min | Serves: 8

Ingredient:

- 200g unsalted butter, softened
- 200g caster sugar
- 4 large eggs
- 200g self-raising flour
- 1 tsp baking powder
- 150g fresh raspberries
- 50g icing sugar
- 200g double cream

Instruction:

1. In a large mixing bowl, cream together the softened butter and caster sugar until light and fluffy.
2. Add the eggs one at a time, beating well after each addition.
3. Sift in the self-raising flour and baking powder. Fold into the batter until just combined.
4. Line the base of your air fryer basket with parchment paper.
5. Pour half of the batter into the air fryer basket, spreading it evenly.
6. In a separate bowl, mash the raspberries with the icing sugar to create a ripple sauce. Spoon this sauce over the batter in the air fryer basket.
7. Drop spoonfuls of the remaining cake batter on top of the raspberry sauce.
8. Use a skewer or knife to create a marbled effect by swirling the batter and raspberry sauce together.
9. Cook the cake in the air fryer at 160°C for 25-30 minutes or until a skewer inserted into the center comes out clean.
10. While the cake is cooling, whip the double cream until soft peaks form.
11. Once the cake is completely cool, top it with the whipped cream and fresh raspberries. Slice and serve **Raspberry Ripple Cake**.

Instruction:

1. In a large mixing bowl, cream together the softened butter and caster sugar until light and fluffy.
2. Add the eggs one at a time, beating well after each addition.
3. Sift in the self-raising flour and baking powder. Add the lemon zest and poppy seeds. Fold into the batter until just combined.
4. Add the lemon juice and whole milk to the batter. Mix until smooth.
5. Line the base of your air fryer basket with parchment paper.
6. Pour the batter into the air fryer basket, spreading it evenly.
7. Cook the cake in the air fryer at 160°C for 25-30 minutes or until a skewer inserted into the center comes out clean.
8. Allow the cake to cool completely in the air fryer basket.
9. Once cooled, carefully remove the cake from the basket and transfer it to a serving plate.
10. Optional: Drizzle a simple lemon glaze on top by mixing icing sugar with lemon juice until smooth.
11. Slice and serve **Lemon Poppy Seed Cake**.

Lemon Poppy Seed Cake

Prep: 15 Min | Cook: 30 Min | Serves: 8

Ingredient:

- 200g unsalted butter, softened
- 200g caster sugar
- 4 large eggs
- 200g self-raising flour
- 1 tsp baking powder
- Zest of 2 lemons
- Juice of 1 lemon
- 1 tbsp poppy seeds
- 150ml whole milk

Chocolate Cherry Cake

Prep: 20 Min | Cook: 35 Min | Serves: 8

Ingredient:

- 200g unsalted butter, softened
- 200g caster sugar
- 4 large eggs
- 200g self-raising flour
- 50g cocoa powder
- 1 tsp baking powder
- 150g dark chocolate, melted
- 1 tsp vanilla extract
- 200g canned cherries, drained and halved

Instruction:

1. In a large mixing bowl, cream together the softened butter and caster sugar until light and fluffy.
2. Add the eggs one at a time, beating well after each addition.
3. Sift in the self-raising flour, cocoa powder, and baking powder. Fold into the batter until just combined.
4. Add the melted dark chocolate and vanilla extract to the batter. Mix until smooth.
5. Line the base of your air fryer basket with parchment paper.
6. Pour half of the batter into the air fryer basket, spreading it out evenly.
7. Place the halved cherries on top of the batter in a single layer.
8. Spoon the remaining batter over the cherries, covering them completely.
9. Cook the cake in the air fryer at 160°C for 30-35 minutes or until a skewer inserted into the center comes out clean.
10. Allow the cake to cool completely in the air fryer basket.
11. Once cooled, carefully remove the cake from the basket and transfer it to a serving plate. Slice and serve **Chocolate Cherry Cake**.

Saffron and Honey Cake

Prep: 20 Min | Cook: 15 Min | Serves: 6

Ingredient:

For the Cake:
- 200g unsalted butter, softened
- 200g caster sugar
- 4 large eggs
- 200g self-raising flour
- A pinch of saffron strands
- 1 tsp baking powder
- 2 tbsp honey
- Zest of 1 orange

For the Glaze:
- 150g icing sugar
- 2 tbsp honey
- Orange zest for garnish (optional)

Instruction:

1. In a small bowl, soak saffron strands in 2 tbsp hot water and set aside.
2. In a large mixing bowl, cream together softened butter and caster sugar until light and fluffy.
3. Add the eggs one at a time, beating well after each addition.
4. In a separate bowl, sift together self-raising flour and baking powder. Gradually fold the flour mixture into the wet ingredients until well combined.
5. Stir in the saffron-infused water, honey, and orange zest to the batter. Grease and line the base of the air fryer basket with parchment paper.
6. Pour the cake batter into the prepared basket, spreading it evenly.
7. Place the air fryer basket in the air fryer. Cook at 160°C for 15 minutes or until a skewer inserted into the centre comes out clean.
8. While the cake is cooking, prepare the glaze by mixing icing sugar and honey until smooth.
9. Once the Saffron and Honey Cake is cooked, remove the basket from the air fryer and let it cool for a few minutes. Drizzle the honey glaze over the warm cake and garnish with orange zest if desired.

Chapter 02: Cakes

Mango and Coconut Cake

Prep: 20 Min | Cook: 35 Min | Serves: 8

Ingredient:

- 200g unsalted butter, softened
- 200g caster sugar
- 4 large eggs
- 200g self-raising flour
- 100g desiccated coconut
- 1 tsp baking powder
- 1 ripe mango, peeled and diced
- 1 tsp vanilla extract
- 150ml coconut milk

Instruction:

1. In a large mixing bowl, cream together the softened butter and caster sugar until light and fluffy.
2. Add the eggs one at a time, beating well after each addition.
3. Sift in the self-raising flour and baking powder. Add the desiccated coconut. Fold into the batter until just combined.
4. Add the diced mango and vanilla extract to the batter. Mix until evenly distributed.
5. Gradually add the coconut milk to the batter, mixing until smooth.
6. Line the base of your air fryer basket with parchment paper.
7. Pour the batter into the air fryer basket, spreading it evenly.
8. Cook the cake in the air fryer at 160°C for 30-35 minutes or until a skewer inserted into the center comes out clean.
9. Allow the cake to cool completely in the air fryer basket.
10. Once cooled, carefully remove the cake from the basket and transfer it to a serving plate. Optionally, top with additional diced mango or a sprinkle of desiccated coconut.
11. Slice and serve **Mango and Coconut Cake**.

Chocolate Hazelnut Cake

Prep: 20 Min | Cook: 35 Min | Serves: 8

Ingredient:

- 200g unsalted butter, softened
- 200g caster sugar
- 4 large eggs
- 200g self-raising flour
- 50g cocoa powder
- 1 tsp baking powder
- 100g hazelnuts, finely chopped
- 150g dark chocolate, melted
- 1 tsp vanilla extract
- 150ml whole milk

Instruction:

1. In a large mixing bowl, cream together the softened butter and caster sugar until light and fluffy.
2. Add the eggs one at a time, beating well after each addition.
3. Sift in the self-raising flour, cocoa powder, and baking powder. Add the finely chopped hazelnuts. Fold into the batter until just combined.
4. Add the melted dark chocolate and vanilla extract to the batter. Mix until smooth.
5. Gradually add the whole milk to the batter, mixing until well incorporated.
6. Line the base of your air fryer basket with parchment paper.
7. Pour the batter into the air fryer basket, spreading it evenly.
8. Cook the cake in the air fryer at 160°C for 30-35 minutes or until a skewer inserted into the center comes out clean.
9. Allow the cake to cool completely in the air fryer basket.
10. Once cooled, carefully remove the cake from the basket and transfer it to a serving plate.
11. Optionally, dust the top of the cake with cocoa powder or icing sugar. Slice and serve **Chocolate Hazelnut Cake**.

Mint Chocolate Chip Cake

Prep: 25 Min | Cook: 30 Min | Serves: 8

Ingredient:

- 200g self-raising flour
- 200g unsalted butter, softened
- 200g caster sugar
- 4 large eggs
- 1 tsp mint extract
- A few drops of green food coloring (optional)
- 100g dark chocolate chips
- 150g double cream

Instruction:

1. In a large mixing bowl, cream together the softened butter and caster sugar until light and fluffy.
2. Add the eggs, one at a time, beating well after each addition. Stir in the mint extract.
3. Gradually add the self-raising flour to the mixture, folding gently until well combined. If desired, add a few drops of green food coloring to achieve a minty hue.
4. Fold in the dark chocolate chips, ensuring they are evenly distributed throughout the batter.
5. Grease a round cake tin that fits inside your air fryer with a little butter or line it with parchment paper. Pour the cake batter into the tin, spreading it out evenly.
6. Place the cake tin in the air fryer basket. Set air fryer at 150°C and cook for 30 minutes.
7. Cool cake, then whip cream until soft peaks form. Spread whipped cream on the cake. Garnish with mint leaves if desired.
8. Slice and serve the delicious **Mint Chocolate Chip Cake.**

Instruction:

1. In a large mixing bowl, cream together the softened butter and caster sugar until light and fluffy.
2. Add the eggs one at a time, beating well after each addition.
3. Sift in the self-raising flour and baking powder. Add the desiccated coconut. Fold into the batter until just combined.
4. Add the diced mango and vanilla extract to the batter. Mix until evenly distributed.
5. Gradually add the coconut milk to the batter, mixing until smooth.
6. Grease the bundt cake mold and place it in the air fryer basket.
7. Pour the batter into the bundt cake mold, spreading it evenly.
8. Cook the cake in the air fryer at 160°C for 35-40 minutes or until a skewer inserted into the center comes out clean.
9. Allow the cake to cool in the bundt cake mold for 10 minutes, then transfer it to a wire rack to cool completely.
10. Once cooled, optionally drizzle with a simple glaze made with icing sugar and a little coconut milk.
11. Slice and serve **Coconut Mango Bundt Cake.**

Coconut Mango Bundt Cake

Prep: 20 Min | Cook: 40 Min | Serves: 8

Ingredient:

- 200g unsalted butter, softened
- 200g caster sugar
- 4 large eggs
- 200g self-raising flour
- 100g desiccated coconut
- 1 tsp baking powder
- 1 ripe mango, peeled and diced
- 1 tsp vanilla extract
- 150ml coconut milk

Chapter 02: Cakes

Pistachio Cranberry Cake

Prep: 20 Min | Cook: 35 Min | Serves: 8

Ingredient:

- 200g unsalted butter, softened
- 200g caster sugar
- 4 large eggs
- 200g self-raising flour
- 100g shelled pistachios, finely chopped
- 1 tsp baking powder
- 100g dried cranberries
- 1 tsp vanilla extract
- 150ml whole milk

Instruction:

1. In a large mixing bowl, cream together the softened butter and caster sugar until light and fluffy.
2. Add the eggs one at a time, beating well after each addition.
3. Sift in the self-raising flour and baking powder. Add the chopped pistachios. Fold into the batter until just combined.
4. Add the dried cranberries and vanilla extract to the batter. Mix until evenly distributed.
5. Gradually add the whole milk to the batter, mixing until smooth.
6. Grease the cake pan and place it in the air fryer basket.
7. Pour the batter into the cake pan, spreading it evenly.
8. Cook the cake in the air fryer at 160°C for 30-35 minutes or until a skewer inserted into the center comes out clean.
9. Allow the cake to cool in the pan for 10 minutes, then transfer it to a wire rack to cool completely.
10. Once cooled, optionally dust the top of the cake with icing sugar or decorate with additional pistachios.
11. Slice and serve **Pistachio Cranberry Cake**.

Instruction:

1. In a large mixing bowl, cream together the softened butter and caster sugar until light and fluffy.
2. Add the eggs one at a time, beating well after each addition.
3. Sift in the self-raising flour, cocoa powder, and baking powder. Fold into the batter until just combined.
4. Add the vanilla extract and whole milk to the batter. Mix until smooth.
5. Line the base of your air fryer basket with parchment paper.
6. Pour half of the batter into the air fryer basket, spreading it out evenly.
7. Place fresh raspberries on top of the batter.
8. Spoon the remaining batter over the raspberries, covering them completely.
9. Use a skewer or knife to create a marbled effect by swirling the batter and raspberries together.
10. Cook the cake in the air fryer at 160°C for 30-35 minutes or until a skewer inserted into the center comes out clean.
11. Allow the cake to cool completely in the air fryer basket. Once cooled, carefully remove the cake and transfer it to a serving plate. Slice and serve **Chocolate Raspberry Cake**.

Chocolate Raspberry Cake

Prep: 20 Min | Cook: 35 Min | Serves: 8

Ingredient:

- 200g unsalted butter, softened
- 200g caster sugar
- 4 large eggs
- 200g self-raising flour
- 50g cocoa powder
- 1 tsp baking powder
- 150g fresh raspberries
- 1 tsp vanilla extract
- 150ml whole milk

Chapter 02: Cakes

Ginger Molasses Cake

Prep: 20 Min | Cook: 40 Min | Serves: 8

Ingredient:

- 200g unsalted butter, softened
- 200g golden syrup
- 200g black treacle
- 200g plain flour
- 1 1/2 tsp ground ginger
- 1 tsp ground cinnamon
- 1/2 tsp ground cloves
- 1/2 tsp baking soda
- 150ml whole milk
- 2 large eggs, beaten
- Icing sugar for dusting (optional)

Instruction:

1. In a saucepan over low heat, melt together the butter, golden syrup, and black treacle. Let it cool slightly.
2. In a large mixing bowl, sift together the flour, ground ginger, ground cinnamon, ground cloves, and baking soda.
3. Pour the melted mixture over the dry ingredients, and mix well.
4. Add the whole milk gradually, stirring continuously to ensure a smooth batter.
5. Add the beaten eggs to the batter and mix until well combined.
6. Line the base of your air fryer basket with parchment paper.
7. Pour the batter into the air fryer basket, spreading it out evenly.
8. Cook the cake in the air fryer at 160°C for 35-40 minutes or until a skewer inserted into the center comes out clean.
9. Allow the cake to cool completely in the air fryer basket.
10. Once cooled, carefully remove the cake and transfer it to a serving plate. Optionally, dust the top with icing sugar.
11. Slice and serve **Ginger Molasses Cake.**

Lemon Elderflower Cake

Prep: 20 Min | Cook: 35 Min | Serves: 8

Ingredient:

- 200g unsalted butter, softened
- 200g caster sugar
- 4 large eggs
- 200g self-raising flour
- 1 tsp baking powder
- Zest of 2 lemons
- 3 tbsp elderflower cordial
- 150g icing sugar
- Juice of 1 lemon
- Fresh edible flowers for decoration (optional)

Instruction:

1. In a large mixing bowl, cream together the softened butter and caster sugar until light and fluffy.
2. Add the eggs one at a time, beating well after each addition.
3. Sift in the self-raising flour and baking powder. Add the lemon zest. Fold into the batter until just combined.
4. Add the elderflower cordial to the batter. Mix until smooth.
5. Line the base of your air fryer basket with parchment paper.
6. Pour the batter into the air fryer basket, spreading it evenly.
7. Cook the cake in the air fryer at 160°C for 30-35 minutes or until a skewer inserted into the center comes out clean.
8. While the cake is cooking, prepare the icing by combining the icing sugar with the lemon juice.
9. Once the cake is cool, drizzle the lemon icing over the top.
10. Optionally, decorate with fresh edible flowers for a touch of elegance.
11. Slice and serve **Lemon Elderflower Cake.**

Chapter 02: Cakes

Chocolate Zucchini Cake

Prep: 20 Min | Cook: 40 Min | Serves: 8

Ingredient:

- 200g self-raising flour
- 50g cocoa powder
- 1 tsp baking powder
- 150g unsalted butter, softened
- 200g caster sugar
- 3 large eggs
- 1 tsp vanilla extract
- 200g grated zucchini, squeezed to remove excess moisture
- 100g dark chocolate, melted
- 150ml whole milk
- Icing sugar for dusting (optional)

Instruction:

1. In a large mixing bowl, sift together the self-raising flour, cocoa powder, and baking powder.
2. In another bowl, cream together the softened butter and caster sugar until light and fluffy.
3. Add the eggs one at a time, beating well after each addition. Stir in the vanilla extract.
4. Gradually add the dry ingredients to the wet ingredients, mixing until just combined.
5. Fold in the grated zucchini, melted dark chocolate, and whole milk until the batter is smooth.
6. Line the base of your air fryer basket with parchment paper.
7. Pour the batter into the air fryer basket, spreading it out evenly.
8. Cook the cake in the air fryer at 160°C for 35-40 minutes or until a skewer inserted into the center comes out clean.
9. Allow the cake to cool completely in the air fryer basket.
10. Once cooled, carefully remove the cake and transfer it to a serving plate. Optionally, dust the top with icing sugar.
11. Slice and serve **Chocolate Zucchini Cake**.

Instruction:

1. In a large mixing bowl, sift together the self-raising flour, cocoa powder, and baking powder.
2. In another bowl, cream together the softened butter and caster sugar until light and fluffy.
3. Add the eggs one at a time, beating well after each addition. Stir in the vanilla extract.
4. Gradually add the dry ingredients to the wet ingredients, mixing until just combined.
5. Fold in the melted dark chocolate and red wine until the batter is smooth.
6. Line the base of your air fryer basket with parchment paper.
7. Pour the batter into the air fryer basket, spreading it out evenly.
8. Cook the cake in the air fryer at 160°C for 35-40 minutes or until a skewer inserted into the center comes out clean.
9. Allow the cake to cool completely in the air fryer basket.
10. Once cooled, carefully remove the cake and transfer it to a serving plate. Optionally, dust the top with icing sugar.
11. Slice and serve **Red Wine Chocolate Cake**.

Red Wine Chocolate Cake

Prep: 20 Min | Cook: 40 Min | Serves: 8

Ingredient:

- 200g self-raising flour
- 50g cocoa powder
- 1 tsp baking powder
- 150g unsalted butter, softened
- 200g caster sugar
- 3 large eggs
- 1 tsp vanilla extract
- 150ml red wine
- 100g dark chocolate, melted
- Icing sugar for dusting (optional)

Hazelnut Muffins

Prep: 15 Min | Cook: 15 Min | Serves: 12 muffins

Ingredient:

- 200g self-raising flour
- 100g caster sugar
- 100g chopped hazelnuts
- 1 tsp baking powder
- 150ml whole milk
- 100g unsalted butter, melted
- 2 large eggs
- 1 tsp vanilla extract
- Pinch of salt
- Icing sugar for dusting (optional)

Instruction:

1. In a large mixing bowl, combine the self-raising flour, caster sugar, chopped hazelnuts, baking powder, and a pinch of salt.
2. In a separate bowl, whisk together the melted butter, eggs, vanilla extract, and whole milk.
3. Pour the wet ingredients into the dry ingredients and gently fold until just combined. Do not overmix.
4. Line the air fryer muffin cups with paper liners.
5. Spoon the batter into the muffin cups, filling each about 2/3 full.
6. Place the muffin cups in the air fryer basket. Be sure to leave some space between each cup for even cooking.
7. Cook the muffins in the air fryer at 180°C for 12-15 minutes or until a toothpick inserted into the center comes out clean.
8. Allow the muffins to cool in the air fryer for a few minutes.
9. Once cooled, carefully remove the muffins from the air fryer and transfer them to a wire rack to cool completely.
10. Optionally, dust the muffins with icing sugar before serving.
11. Serve and enjoy the **Hazelnut Muffins**!

Instruction:

1. In a small saucepan, warm the milk until just below boiling. Add the Earl Grey tea bags and steep for 5 minutes. Remove the tea bags and let the milk cool to room temperature.
2. In a large mixing bowl, combine the self-raising flour, caster sugar, baking powder, and a pinch of salt.
3. In a separate bowl, whisk together the melted butter, eggs, vanilla extract, and the cooled Earl Grey-infused milk.
4. Pour the wet ingredients into the dry ingredients and gently fold until just combined. Do not overmix.
5. Line the air fryer muffin cups with paper liners.
6. Spoon the batter into the muffin cups, filling each about 2/3 full.
7. Place the muffin cups in the air fryer basket. Be sure to leave some space between each cup for even cooking.
8. Cook the muffins in the air fryer at 180°C for 12-15 minutes or until a toothpick inserted into the center comes out clean.
9. Allow the muffins to cool in the air fryer for a few minutes.
10. Once cooled, carefully remove the muffins from the air fryer and transfer them to a wire rack to cool completely.
11. Optionally, dust the muffins with icing sugar before serving **Earl Grey Muffins**!

Earl Grey Muffins

Prep: 20 Min | Cook: 15 Min | Serves: 12 muffins

Ingredient:

- 200g self-raising flour
- 100g caster sugar
- 2 Earl Grey tea bags
- 150ml whole milk
- 100g unsalted butter, melted
- 2 large eggs
- 1 tsp baking powder
- 1 tsp vanilla extract
- Pinch of salt
- Icing sugar for dusting (optional)

Chapter 03: Muffins

Almond Joy Muffins

Prep: 20 Min | Cook: 15 Min | Serves: 12 muffins

Ingredient:

- 200g self-raising flour
- 100g caster sugar
- 100g unsalted butter, melted
- 150ml whole milk
- 2 large eggs
- 1 tsp almond extract
- 100g desiccated coconut
- 75g chopped almonds
- 100g dark chocolate chips
- A pinch of salt
- Flaked coconut and whole almonds for topping (optional)

Instruction:

1. In a large mixing bowl, combine the self-raising flour, caster sugar, desiccated coconut, chopped almonds, dark chocolate chips, and a pinch of salt.
2. In a separate bowl, whisk together the melted butter, whole milk, eggs, and almond extract.
3. Pour the wet ingredients into the dry ingredients and gently fold until just combined. Do not overmix.
4. Line the air fryer muffin cups with paper liners.
5. Spoon the batter into the muffin cups, filling each about 2/3 full.
6. Place the muffin cups in the air fryer basket. Be sure to leave some space between each cup for even cooking.
7. Cook the muffins in the air fryer at 180°C for 12-15 minutes or until a toothpick inserted into the center comes out clean.
8. Allow the muffins to cool in the air fryer for a few minutes.
9. Once cooled, carefully remove the muffins from the air fryer and transfer them to a wire rack to cool completely.
10. Optionally, top each muffin with flaked coconut and a whole almond for decoration.
11. Serve and enjoy **Almond Joy Muffins**!

Instruction:

1. In a large mixing bowl, whisk together the self-raising flour, light brown sugar, ground ginger, ground cinnamon, ground nutmeg, ground cloves, and a pinch of salt.
2. In a separate bowl, combine the melted butter, whole milk, black treacle, egg, and vanilla extract. Mix until well combined.
3. Pour the wet ingredients into the dry ingredients and gently fold until just combined. Do not overmix.
4. Line the air fryer muffin cups with paper liners.
5. Spoon the batter into the muffin cups, filling each about 2/3 full.
6. Place the muffin cups in the air fryer basket. Be sure to leave some space between each cup for even cooking.
7. Cook the muffins in the air fryer at 180°C for 12-15 minutes or until a toothpick inserted into the center comes out clean.
8. Allow the muffins to cool in the air fryer for a few minutes.
9. Once cooled, carefully remove the muffins from the air fryer and transfer them to a wire rack to cool completely.
10. Optionally, dust the muffins with icing sugar before serving.
11. Serve and enjoy **Gingerbread Muffins**!

Gingerbread Muffins

Prep: 20 Min | Cook: 15 Min | Serves: 12 muffins

Ingredient:

- 200g self-raising flour
- 100g light brown sugar
- 1 tsp ground ginger
- 1/2 tsp ground cinnamon
- 1/4 tsp ground nutmeg
- 1/4 tsp ground cloves
- 100g unsalted butter, melted
- 150ml whole milk
- 2 tbsp black treacle
- 1 large egg
- 1 tsp vanilla extract
- A pinch of salt
- Icing sugar for dusting (optional)

Chapter 03: Muffins

Maple Bacon Muffins

Prep: 20 Min | Cook: 15 Min | Serves: 12 muffins

Ingredient:

- 200g self-raising flour
- 100g caster sugar
- 100g unsalted butter, melted
- 150ml whole milk
- 2 large eggs
- 4 rashers of streaky bacon, cooked and chopped
- 3 tbsp maple syrup
- 1 tsp baking powder
- 1 tsp vanilla extract
- A pinch of salt
- Icing sugar for dusting (optional)

Instruction:

1. In a large mixing bowl, whisk together the self-raising flour, caster sugar, baking powder, and a pinch of salt.
2. In a separate bowl, combine the melted butter, whole milk, eggs, maple syrup, and vanilla extract. Mix until well combined.
3. Pour the wet ingredients into the dry ingredients and gently fold until just combined. Do not overmix.
4. Line the air fryer muffin cups with paper liners.
5. Spoon the batter into the muffin cups, filling each about 2/3 full.
6. Sprinkle the chopped bacon evenly over the muffin batter.
7. Place the muffin cups in the air fryer basket. Be sure to leave some space between each cup for even cooking.
8. Cook the muffins in the air fryer at 180°C for 12-15 minutes or until a toothpick inserted into the center comes out clean.
9. Allow the muffins to cool in the air fryer for a few minutes.
10. Once cooled, carefully remove the muffins from the air fryer and transfer them to a wire rack to cool completely.
11. Optionally, dust the muffins with icing sugar before serving **Maple Bacon Muffins**.

Apple Cider Muffins

Prep: 20 Min | Cook: 15 Min | Serves: 12 muffins

Ingredient:

- 200g self-raising flour
- 100g light brown sugar
- 100g unsalted butter, melted
- 150ml apple cider
- 2 large eggs
- 1 tsp ground cinnamon
- 1/2 tsp ground nutmeg
- 1 tsp baking powder
- 1 tsp vanilla extract
- 1 large apple, peeled, cored, and diced
- A pinch of salt
- Icing sugar for dusting (optional)

Instruction:

1. In a large mixing bowl, whisk together the self-raising flour, light brown sugar, ground cinnamon, ground nutmeg, baking powder, and a pinch of salt.
2. In a separate bowl, combine the melted butter, apple cider, eggs, and vanilla extract. Mix until well combined.
3. Pour the wet ingredients into the dry ingredients and gently fold until just combined. Do not overmix.
4. Fold in the diced apple into the batter.
5. Line the air fryer muffin cups with paper liners.
6. Spoon the batter into the muffin cups, filling each about 2/3 full.
7. Place the muffin cups in the air fryer basket. Be sure to leave some space between each cup for even cooking.
8. Cook the muffins in the air fryer at 180°C for 12-15 minutes or until a toothpick inserted into the center comes out clean.
9. Allow the muffins to cool in the air fryer for a few minutes.
10. Once cooled, carefully remove the muffins from the air fryer and transfer them to a wire rack to cool completely.
11. Optionally, dust the muffins with icing sugar before serving **Apple Cider Muffins**.

Chapter 03: Muffins

Apple Walnut Muffins

Prep: 20 Min | Cook: 15 Min | Serves: 12 muffins

Ingredient:

- 200g self-raising flour
- 100g caster sugar
- 1 tsp baking powder
- 1/2 tsp ground cinnamon
- 1/4 tsp salt
- 1 large egg
- 180ml milk
- 80ml vegetable oil
- 1 tsp vanilla extract
- 1 large apple, peeled, cored, and diced
- 50g walnuts, chopped

Instruction:

1. In a mixing bowl, combine the self-raising flour, caster sugar, baking powder, ground cinnamon, and salt. In a separate bowl, whisk together the egg, milk, vegetable oil, and vanilla extract. Pour the wet ingredients into the dry ingredients and mix until just combined. Do not overmix; lumps are okay.
2. Gently fold in the diced apple and chopped walnuts.
3. Line a muffin pan with paper liners or grease the muffin cups. Divide the muffin batter evenly among the cups, filling each about 2/3 full.
4. Place the muffin pan into the air fryer basket, ensuring there is enough space around it for air circulation. Cook the muffins in the air fryer at 180°C for approximately 15 minutes or until a toothpick inserted into the center comes out clean.
5. Once cooked, remove the muffins from the air fryer and let them cool in the pan for a few minutes. Transfer the muffins to a wire rack to cool completely.
6. Enjoy your delicious **Apple Walnut Muffins**, filled with the delightful combination of apples and walnuts!

Maple Walnut Muffins

Prep: 20 Min | Cook: 15 Min | Serves: 12 muffins

Ingredient:

- 200g self-raising flour
- 100g light brown sugar
- 100g unsalted butter, melted
- 150ml whole milk
- 2 large eggs
- 3 tbsp maple syrup
- 100g chopped walnuts
- 1 tsp baking powder
- 1 tsp vanilla extract
- A pinch of salt
- Icing sugar for dusting (optional)

Instruction:

1. In a large mixing bowl, whisk together the self-raising flour, light brown sugar, chopped walnuts, baking powder, and a pinch of salt.
2. In a separate bowl, combine the melted butter, whole milk, eggs, maple syrup, and vanilla extract. Mix until well combined.
3. Pour the wet ingredients into the dry ingredients and gently fold until just combined. Do not overmix.
4. Line the air fryer muffin cups with paper liners.
5. Spoon the batter into the muffin cups, filling each about 2/3 full.
6. Place the muffin cups in the air fryer basket. Be sure to leave some space between each cup for even cooking.
7. Cook the muffins in the air fryer at 180°C for 12-15 minutes or until a toothpick inserted into the center comes out clean.
8. Allow the muffins to cool in the air fryer for a few minutes.
9. Once cooled, carefully remove the muffins from the air fryer and transfer them to a wire rack to cool completely.
10. Optionally, dust the muffins with icing sugar before serving.
11. Serve and enjoy **Maple Walnut Muffins**!

Mango Banana Muffins

Prep: 20 Min | Cook: 15 Min | Serves: 12 muffins

Ingredient:

- 200g self-raising flour
- 100g caster sugar
- 100g unsalted butter, melted
- 2 ripe bananas, mashed
- 1 ripe mango, peeled, pitted, and diced
- 2 large eggs
- 1 tsp vanilla extract
- 1 tsp baking powder
- 1/2 tsp ground cinnamon
- A pinch of salt
- Icing sugar for dusting (optional)

Instruction:

1. In a large mixing bowl, whisk together the self-raising flour, caster sugar, baking powder, ground cinnamon, and a pinch of salt.
2. In a separate bowl, combine the melted butter, mashed bananas, diced mango, eggs, and vanilla extract. Mix until well combined.
3. Pour the wet ingredients into the dry ingredients and gently fold until just combined. Do not overmix.
4. Line the air fryer muffin cups with paper liners.
5. Spoon the batter into the muffin cups, filling each about 2/3 full.
6. Place the muffin cups in the air fryer basket. Be sure to leave some space between each cup for even cooking.
7. Cook the muffins in the air fryer at 180°C for 12-15 minutes or until a toothpick inserted into the center comes out clean.
8. Allow the muffins to cool in the air fryer for a few minutes.
9. Once cooled, carefully remove the muffins from the air fryer and transfer them to a wire rack to cool completely.
10. Optionally, dust the muffins with icing sugar before serving.
11. Serve and enjoy **Mango Banana Muffins**!

Instruction:

1. In a mixing bowl, combine the self-raising flour, caster sugar, baking powder, and salt. In a separate bowl, whisk together the egg, milk, vegetable oil, orange zest, orange juice, and grated ginger. Pour the wet ingredients into the dry ingredients and mix until just combined. Do not overmix; lumps are okay.
2. Line a muffin pan with paper liners or grease the muffin cups. Divide the muffin batter evenly among the cups, filling each about 2/3 full.
3. Place the muffin pan into the air fryer basket, ensuring there is enough space around it for air circulation.
4. Cook the muffins in the air fryer at 180°C for approximately 15 minutes or until a toothpick inserted into the center comes out clean.
5. Once cooked, remove the muffins from the air fryer and let them cool in the pan for a few minutes. Transfer the muffins to a wire rack to cool completely.
6. Enjoy your delicious **Orange Ginger Muffins**, infused with the bright flavors of orange and ginger!

Orange Ginger Muffins

Prep: 15 Min | Cook: 15 Min | Serves: 12 muffins

Ingredient:

- 250g self-raising flour
- 100g caster sugar
- 1 tsp baking powder
- 1/4 tsp salt
- 1 large egg
- 180ml milk
- 80ml vegetable oil
- Zest of 1 orange
- 1 tbsp freshly squeezed orange juice
- 1 tbsp grated fresh ginger

Chapter 03: Muffins

Peach Cobbler Muffins

Prep: 20 Min | Cook: 15 Min | Serves: 12 muffins

Ingredient:

- 200g self-raising flour
- 100g caster sugar
- 100g unsalted butter, melted
- 2 large eggs
- 150ml whole milk
- 2 ripe peaches, peeled, pitted, and diced
- 1 tsp vanilla extract
- 1 tsp baking powder
- 1/2 tsp ground cinnamon
- A pinch of salt
- Demerara sugar for topping (optional)

Instruction:

1. In a large mixing bowl, whisk together the self-raising flour, caster sugar, baking powder, ground cinnamon, and a pinch of salt.
2. In a separate bowl, combine the melted butter, eggs, whole milk, diced peaches, and vanilla extract. Mix until well combined.
3. Pour the wet ingredients into the dry ingredients and gently fold until just combined. Do not overmix.
4. Line the air fryer muffin cups with paper liners.
5. Spoon the batter into the muffin cups, filling each about 2/3 full.
6. Optionally, sprinkle a little Demerara sugar on top of each muffin for a sweet crunch.
7. Place the muffin cups in the air fryer basket. Be sure to leave some space between each cup for even cooking.
8. Cook the muffins in the air fryer at 180°C for 12-15 minutes or until a toothpick inserted into the center comes out clean.
9. Allow the muffins to cool in the air fryer for a few minutes.
10. Once cooled, carefully remove the muffins from the air fryer and transfer them to a wire rack to cool completely.
11. Serve and enjoy **Peach Cobbler Muffins!**

Instruction:

1. In a large mixing bowl, whisk together the self-raising flour, caster sugar, baking powder, desiccated coconut, and a pinch of salt.
2. In a separate bowl, combine the melted butter, coconut milk, eggs, diced mangoes, and vanilla extract. Mix until well combined.
3. Pour the wet ingredients into the dry ingredients and gently fold until just combined. Do not overmix.
4. Line the air fryer muffin cups with paper liners.
5. Spoon the batter into the muffin cups, filling each about 2/3 full.
6. Place the muffin cups in the air fryer basket. Be sure to leave some space between each cup for even cooking.
7. Cook the muffins in the air fryer at 180°C for 12-15 minutes or until a toothpick inserted into the center comes out clean.
8. Allow the muffins to cool in the air fryer for a few minutes.
9. Once cooled, carefully remove the muffins from the air fryer and transfer them to a wire rack to cool completely.
10. Optionally, dust the muffins with icing sugar before serving.
11. Serve and enjoy **Mango Coconut Muffins!**

Mango Coconut Muffins

Prep: 20 Min | Cook: 15 Min | Serves: 12 muffins

Ingredient:

- 200g self-raising flour
- 100g caster sugar
- 100g unsalted butter, melted
- 150ml coconut milk
- 2 ripe mangoes, peeled, pitted, and diced
- 2 large eggs
- 1 tsp vanilla extract
- 1 tsp baking powder
- 50g desiccated coconut
- A pinch of salt
- Icing sugar for dusting (optional)

Pumpkin Pecan Muffins

Prep: 20 Min | Cook: 15 Min | Serves: 12 muffins

Ingredient:

- 200g self-raising flour
- 100g light brown sugar
- 100g unsalted butter, melted
- 150g canned pumpkin puree
- 2 large eggs
- 1 tsp ground cinnamon
- 1/2 tsp ground ginger
- 1/4 tsp ground nutmeg
- 1/4 tsp ground cloves
- 100g chopped pecans
- 1 tsp baking powder
- A pinch of salt
- Icing sugar for dusting (optional)

Instruction:

1. In a large mixing bowl, whisk together the self-raising flour, light brown sugar, ground cinnamon, ground ginger, ground nutmeg, ground cloves, baking powder, chopped pecans, and a pinch of salt.
2. In a separate bowl, combine the melted butter, pumpkin puree, eggs, and vanilla extract. Mix until well combined.
3. Pour the wet ingredients into the dry ingredients and gently fold until just combined. Do not overmix.
4. Line the air fryer muffin cups with paper liners.
5. Spoon the batter into the muffin cups, filling each about 2/3 full.
6. Place the muffin cups in the air fryer basket. Be sure to leave some space between each cup for even cooking.
7. Cook the muffins in the air fryer at 180°C for 12-15 minutes or until a toothpick inserted into the center comes out clean.
8. Allow the muffins to cool in the air fryer for a few minutes.
9. Once cooled, carefully remove the muffins from the air fryer and transfer them to a wire rack to cool completely.
10. Optionally, dust the muffins with icing sugar before serving.
11. Serve and enjoy **Pumpkin Pecan Muffins**!

Instruction:

1. In a large mixing bowl, whisk together the self-raising flour, light brown sugar, baking powder, chopped pecans, and a pinch of salt.
2. In a separate bowl, combine the melted butter, whole milk, eggs, and vanilla extract. Mix until well combined.
3. Pour the wet ingredients into the dry ingredients and gently fold until just combined. Do not overmix.
4. Line the air fryer muffin cups with paper liners.
5. Spoon the batter into the muffin cups, filling each about 2/3 full.
6. Create a small well in the center of each muffin and spoon in a dollop of caramel sauce.
7. Use a toothpick or skewer to swirl the caramel into the batter.
8. Place the muffin cups in the air fryer basket. Be sure to leave some space between each cup for even cooking.
9. Cook the muffins in the air fryer at 180°C for 12-15 minutes or until a toothpick inserted into the center comes out clean.
10. Allow the muffins to cool in the air fryer for a few minutes.
11. Once cooled, carefully remove the muffins from the air fryer and transfer them to a wire rack to cool completely.
12. Optionally, dust the muffins with icing sugar before serving **Caramel Pecan Muffins**!

Caramel Pecan Muffins

Prep: 20 Min | Cook: 15 Min | Serves: 12 muffins

Ingredient:

- 200g self-raising flour
- 100g light brown sugar
- 100g unsalted butter, melted
- 150ml whole milk
- 2 large eggs
- 1 tsp vanilla extract
- 100g chopped pecans
- 100g caramel sauce
- 1 tsp baking powder
- A pinch of salt
- Icing sugar for dusting (optional)

Chapter 03: Muffins

Apricot Almond Muffins

Prep: 15 Min | Cook: 15 Min | Serves: 12 muffins

Ingredient:

- 200g self-raising flour
- 100g caster sugar
- 50g ground almonds
- 1 tsp baking powder
- 1/2 tsp baking soda
- 1/4 tsp salt
- 150ml whole milk
- 75ml vegetable oil
- 2 large eggs
- 1 tsp almond extract
- 100g dried apricots, chopped

Instruction:

1. In a mixing bowl, combine the self-raising flour, caster sugar, ground almonds, baking powder, baking soda, and salt.
2. In a separate bowl, whisk together the milk, vegetable oil, eggs, and almond extract.
3. Pour the wet ingredients into the dry ingredients and stir until just combined. Do not overmix.
4. Fold in the chopped dried apricots.
5. Line a muffin tray with paper cases or grease it with a little butter. Fill each muffin case three-quarters full with the batter.
6. Place the muffin tray in the air fryer basket. Set the air fryer temperature to 180°C and the cooking time to 15 minutes.
7. Once the muffins are cooked, carefully remove them from the air fryer and allow them to cool in the tray for a few minutes before transferring them to a wire rack to cool completely.
8. Serve and enjoy the delightful **Apricot Almond Muffins**!

Instruction:

1. In a large mixing bowl, whisk together the self-raising flour, light brown sugar, baking powder, and a pinch of salt.
2. In a separate bowl, combine the melted butter, eggs, whole milk, and vanilla extract. Mix until well combined.
3. Pour the wet ingredients into the dry ingredients and gently fold until just combined. Do not overmix.
4. Fold in the diced apples into the batter.
5. Line the air fryer muffin cups with paper liners.
6. Spoon the batter into the muffin cups, filling each about 2/3 full.
7. In a small bowl, prepare the streusel topping by mixing together the plain flour, light brown sugar, diced cold butter, and ground cinnamon until crumbly.
8. Sprinkle the streusel topping evenly over each muffin.
9. Place the muffin cups in the air fryer basket. Be sure to leave some space between each cup for even cooking.
10. Cook the muffins in the air fryer at 180°C for 12-15 minutes or until a toothpick inserted into the center comes out clean.
11. Allow the muffins to cool in the air fryer for a few minutes.
12. Once cooled, carefully remove the muffins from the air fryer and transfer them to a wire rack to cool completely.
13. Enoy the **Apple Streusel Muffins**.

Apple Streusel Muffins

Prep: 20 Min | Cook: 15 Min | Serves: 12 muffins

Ingredient:

- 200g self-raising flour
- 100g light brown sugar
- 100g unsalted butter, melted
- 2 medium-sized apples, peeled, cored, and diced
- 2 large eggs
- 150ml whole milk
- 1 tsp vanilla extract
- 1 tsp baking powder
- A pinch of salt
- 50g plain flour
- 1 tsp ground cinnamon

Chapter 03: Muffins

Chocolate Mint Muffins

Prep: 15 Min | Cook: 12 Min | Serves: 6 muffins

Ingredient:

- 150g self-raising flour
- 25g cocoa powder
- 100g granulated sugar
- 1/4 tsp salt
- 1 large egg
- 120ml milk
- 60ml vegetable oil
- 1 tsp peppermint extract
- 100g dark chocolate chips
- 100g dark chocolate, melted
- Mint leaves for garnish (optional)

Instruction:

1. n a mixing bowl, whisk together the self-raising flour, cocoa powder, sugar, and salt.
2. In a separate bowl, beat the egg and then add the milk, vegetable oil, and peppermint extract. Mix well.
3. Pour the wet ingredients into the dry ingredients and stir until just combined.
4. Gently fold in the dark chocolate chips.
5. Line the air fryer basket with silicone liners or use silicone muffin cups.
6. Spoon the muffin batter into the lined air fryer basket, filling each cup about 2/3 full.
7. Place the basket in the air fryer. Set the temperature to 180°C and the cooking time to 12 minutes.
8. Once the cooking time is up, carefully remove the muffins from the air fryer and let them cool slightly.
9. For the topping, melt the dark chocolate in a heatproof bowl.
10. Dip the tops of the muffins into the melted chocolate and allow it to set.
11. Optional: Garnish each muffin with a mint leaf. Serve the **Chocolate Mint Muffins** and enjoy!

Instruction:

1. In a mixing bowl, whisk together the cornmeal, plain flour, baking powder, and salt.
2. In a separate bowl, beat the egg and then add the granulated sugar, milk, vegetable oil, and honey. Mix well.
3. Pour the wet ingredients into the dry ingredients and stir until just combined.
4. Line the air fryer basket with silicone liners or use silicone muffin cups.
5. Spoon the muffin batter into the lined air fryer basket, filling each cup about 2/3 full.
6. Place the basket in the air fryer. Set the temperature to 180°C and the cooking time to 12 minutes.
7. Once the cooking time is up, carefully remove the muffins from the air fryer and let them cool slightly.
8. Serve the **Honey Cornbread Muffins** and enjoy!

Honey Cornbread Muffins

Prep: 10 Min | Cook: 12 Min | Serves: 6 muffins

Ingredient:

- 125g cornmeal
- 125g plain flour
- 1 tbsp baking powder
- 1/4 tsp salt
- 1 large egg
- 60g granulated sugar
- 120ml milk
- 60ml vegetable oil
- 2 tbsp honey

Raspberry Swirl Muffins

Prep: 15 Min | Cook: 15 Min | Serves: 6 muffins

Ingredient:

- 175g self-raising flour
- 75g granulated sugar
- 1/4 tsp salt
- 1 large egg
- 125ml milk
- 50ml vegetable oil
- 1 tsp vanilla extract
- 75g fresh raspberries
- 1 tbsp granulated sugar (for raspberry swirl)

Instruction:

1. In a mixing bowl, combine the self-raising flour, granulated sugar, and salt.
2. In a separate bowl, whisk together the egg, milk, vegetable oil, and vanilla extract.
3. Pour the wet ingredients into the dry ingredients and stir until just combined.
4. Line the air fryer basket with silicone liners or use silicone muffin cups.
5. Spoon the muffin batter into the lined air fryer basket, filling each cup about 2/3 full.
6. In a small bowl, mash the fresh raspberries with 1 tablespoon of granulated sugar.
7. Drop small dollops of the raspberry mixture onto the top of each muffin batter.
8. Use a toothpick or skewer to gently swirl the raspberry mixture into the muffin batter, creating a marbled effect.
9. Place the basket in the air fryer. Set the temperature to 180°C and the cooking time to 15 minutes.
10. Once the cooking time is up, carefully remove the muffins from the air fryer and let them cool slightly. Serve the **Raspberry Swirl Muffins** and enjoy!

Instruction:

1. In a mixing bowl, whisk together the self-raising flour, ground ginger, ground cinnamon, ground cloves, and salt.
2. In a separate bowl, mix the melted butter and dark brown sugar until well combined.
3. Add the egg, milk, molasses, and vanilla extract to the butter and sugar mixture. Mix well.
4. Pour the wet ingredients into the dry ingredients and stir until just combined.
5. Line the air fryer basket with silicone liners or use silicone muffin cups.
6. Spoon the muffin batter into the lined air fryer basket, filling each cup about 2/3 full.
7. Place the basket in the air fryer. Set the temperature to 180°C and the cooking time to 15 minutes.
8. Once the cooking time is up, carefully remove the muffins from the air fryer and let them cool slightly. Serve the **Ginger Molasses Muffins** and enjoy!

Ginger Molasses Muffins

Prep: 15 Min | Cook: 15 Min | Serves: 6 muffins

Ingredient:

- 175g self-raising flour
- 1 tsp ground ginger
- 1/2 tsp ground cinnamon
- 1/4 tsp ground cloves
- 1/4 tsp salt
- 75g unsalted butter, melted
- 75g dark brown sugar
- 1 large egg
- 125ml milk
- 60ml molasses
- 1 tsp vanilla extract

Chapter 03: Muffins

Chocolate Orange Muffins

Prep: 15 Min | Cook: 15 Min | Serves: 6 muffins

Ingredient:

- 175g self-raising flour
- 25g cocoa powder
- 1/2 tsp baking powder
- 1/4 tsp salt
- 75g granulated sugar
- Zest of 1 orange
- 1 large egg
- 125ml milk
- 60ml vegetable oil
- 1 tsp vanilla extract
- 100g dark chocolate chips

Instruction:

1. In a mixing bowl, whisk together the self-raising flour, cocoa powder, baking powder, salt, granulated sugar, and orange zest.
2. In a separate bowl, beat the egg, then add the milk, vegetable oil, and vanilla extract. Mix well.
3. Pour the wet ingredients into the dry ingredients and stir until just combined.
4. Gently fold in the dark chocolate chips.
5. Line the air fryer basket with silicone liners or use silicone muffin cups.
6. Spoon the muffin batter into the lined air fryer basket, filling each cup about 2/3 full.
7. Place the basket in the air fryer. Set the temperature to 180°C and the cooking time to 15 minutes.
8. Once the cooking time is up, carefully remove the muffins from the air fryer and let them cool slightly. Serve the **Chocolate Orange Muffins** and enjoy!

Cranberry Walnut Muffins

Prep: 15 Min | Cook: 15 Min | Serves: 6 muffins

Ingredient:

- 175g self-raising flour
- 75g granulated sugar
- 1/4 tsp salt
- 1 large egg
- 125ml milk
- 60ml vegetable oil
- 1 tsp vanilla extract
- 75g dried cranberries
- 50g walnuts, chopped

Instruction:

1. In a mixing bowl, whisk together the self-raising flour, granulated sugar, and salt.
2. In a separate bowl, beat the egg, then add the milk, vegetable oil, and vanilla extract. Mix well.
3. Pour the wet ingredients into the dry ingredients and stir until just combined.
4. Gently fold in the dried cranberries and chopped walnuts.
5. Line the air fryer basket with silicone liners or use silicone muffin cups.
6. Spoon the muffin batter into the lined air fryer basket, filling each cup about 2/3 full.
7. Place the basket in the air fryer. Set the temperature to 180°C and the cooking time to 15 minutes.
8. Once the cooking time is up, carefully remove the muffins from the air fryer and let them cool slightly. Serve the **Cranberry Walnut Muffins** and enjoy!

Chocolate Cherry Muffins

Prep: 15 Min | Cook: 15 Min | Serves: 6 muffins

Ingredient:

- 175g self-raising flour
- 25g cocoa powder
- 1/2 tsp baking powder
- 1/4 tsp salt
- 75g granulated sugar
- 1 large egg
- 125ml milk
- 60ml vegetable oil
- 1 tsp vanilla extract
- 75g dark chocolate, chopped
- 75g cherries, pitted and chopped

Instruction:

1. In a mixing bowl, whisk together the self-raising flour, cocoa powder, baking powder, salt, and granulated sugar.
2. In a separate bowl, beat the egg, then add the milk, vegetable oil, and vanilla extract. Mix well.
3. Pour the wet ingredients into the dry ingredients and stir until just combined.
4. Gently fold in the chopped dark chocolate and cherries.
5. Line the air fryer basket with silicone liners or use silicone muffin cups.
6. Spoon the muffin batter into the lined air fryer basket, filling each cup about 2/3 full.
7. Place the basket in the air fryer. Set the temperature to 180°C and the cooking time to 15 minutes.
8. Once the cooking time is up, carefully remove the muffins from the air fryer and let them cool slightly. Serve the **Chocolate Cherry Muffins** and enjoy!

Instruction:

1. In a mixing bowl, whisk together the self-raising flour, desiccated coconut, granulated sugar, and salt.
2. In a separate bowl, beat the egg, then add the milk, vegetable oil, and vanilla extract. Mix well.
3. Pour the wet ingredients into the dry ingredients and stir until just combined.
4. Gently fold in the fresh raspberries, being careful not to crush them too much.
5. Line the air fryer basket with silicone liners or use silicone muffin cups.
6. Spoon the muffin batter into the lined air fryer basket, filling each cup about 2/3 full.
7. Place the basket in the air fryer. Set the temperature to 180°C and the cooking time to 15 minutes.
8. Once the cooking time is up, carefully remove the muffins from the air fryer and let them cool slightly. Serve the **Coconut Raspberry Muffins** and enjoy!

Coconut Raspberry Muffins

Prep: 15 Min | Cook: 15 Min | Serves: 6 muffins

Ingredient:

- 175g self-raising flour
- 50g desiccated coconut
- 75g granulated sugar
- 1/4 tsp salt
- 1 large egg
- 125ml milk
- 60ml vegetable oil
- 1 tsp vanilla extract
- 75g fresh raspberries

Chapter 03: Muffins

Strawberry Banana Muffins

Prep: 15 Min | Cook: 15 Min | Serves: 6 mufins

Ingredient:

- 175g self-raising flour
- 75g granulated sugar
- 1/4 tsp salt
- 1 large egg
- 125ml milk
- 60ml vegetable oil
- 1 tsp vanilla extract
- 1 ripe banana, mashed
- 75g fresh strawberries, diced

Instruction:

1. In a mixing bowl, whisk together the self-raising flour, granulated sugar, and salt.
2. In a separate bowl, beat the egg, then add the milk, vegetable oil, and vanilla extract. Mix well.
3. Pour the wet ingredients into the dry ingredients and stir until just combined.
4. Gently fold in the mashed banana and diced strawberries.
5. Line the air fryer basket with silicone liners or use silicone muffin cups.
6. Spoon the muffin batter into the lined air fryer basket, filling each cup about 2/3 full.
7. Place the basket in the air fryer. Set the temperature to 180°C and the cooking time to 15 minutes.
8. Once the cooking time is up, carefully remove the muffins from the air fryer and let them cool slightly. Serve the **Strawberry Banana Muffins** and enjoy!

Chocolate Zucchini Muffins

Prep: 15 Min | Cook: 25 Min | Serves: 12 mufins

Ingredient:

- 200g plain flour
- 50g cocoa powder
- 1 tsp baking soda
- 1/2 tsp baking powder
- 1/4 tsp salt
- 125g caster sugar
- 2 large eggs
- 120ml vegetable oil
- 1 tsp vanilla extract
- 200g zucchini (courgette), grated and excess moisture squeezed out
- 100g chocolate chips, plus extra for topping

Instruction:

1. Grate the zucchini and use a clean kitchen towel or paper towels to squeeze out as much moisture as possible.
2. In a large mixing bowl, sift together the plain flour, cocoa powder, baking soda, baking powder, and salt. Stir in the caster sugar.
3. In another bowl, beat the eggs lightly. Mix in the vegetable oil and vanilla extract until well combined.
4. Pour the wet ingredients into the dry ingredients. Stir gently until just combined. Avoid overmixing to ensure the muffins stay tender.
5. Fold in the grated zucchini and chocolate chips until evenly distributed throughout the batter.
6. Line a 12-cup muffin tin with paper liners or lightly grease the cups. Divide the batter evenly among the muffin cups, filling each about 3/4 full. Sprinkle additional chocolate chips on top if desired.
7. Bake:
8. Preheat your air fryer for a few minutes at 160°C if it requires preheating. Place the muffin tin in the air fryer basket. Bake at 160°C for 20-25 minutes, or until a toothpick inserted into the center of a muffin comes out clean.
9. Allow the **Chocolate Zucchini Muffins** to cool in the tin for 5 minutes, then transfer them to a wire rack to cool completely.

Chapter 03: Muffins

Blackberry Vanilla Muffins

Prep: 15 Min | Cook: 15 Min | Serves: 6 mufins

Ingredient:

- 175g self-raising flour
- 75g granulated sugar
- 1/4 tsp salt
- 1 large egg
- 125ml milk
- 60ml vegetable oil
- 1 tsp vanilla extract
- 75g fresh blackberries

Instruction:

1. In a mixing bowl, whisk together the self-raising flour, granulated sugar, and salt.
2. In a separate bowl, beat the egg, then add the milk, vegetable oil, and vanilla extract. Mix well.
3. Pour the wet ingredients into the dry ingredients and stir until just combined.
4. Gently fold in the fresh blackberries, being careful not to crush them too much.
5. Line the air fryer basket with silicone liners or use silicone muffin cups.
6. Spoon the muffin batter into the lined air fryer basket, filling each cup about 2/3 full.
7. Place the basket in the air fryer. Set the temperature to 180°C and the cooking time to 15 minutes.
8. Once the cooking time is up, carefully remove the muffins from the air fryer and let them cool slightly. Serve the **Blackberry Vanilla Muffins** and enjoy!

Instruction:

1. In a mixing bowl, whisk together the self-raising flour, granulated sugar, and salt.
2. In a separate bowl, beat the egg, then add the milk, vegetable oil, and vanilla extract. Mix well.
3. Pour the wet ingredients into the dry ingredients and stir until just combined.
4. Gently fold in the diced strawberries and rhubarb.
5. Line the air fryer basket with silicone liners or use silicone muffin cups.
6. Spoon the muffin batter into the lined air fryer basket, filling each cup about 2/3 full.
7. Place the basket in the air fryer. Set the temperature to 180°C and the cooking time to 15 minutes.
8. Once the cooking time is up, carefully remove the muffins from the air fryer and let them cool slightly. Serve the **Strawberry Rhubarb Muffins** and enjoy!

Strawberry Rhubarb Muffins

Prep: 15 Min | Cook: 15 Min | Serves: 6 mufins

Ingredient:

- 175g self-raising flour
- 75g granulated sugar
- 1/4 tsp salt
- 1 large egg
- 125ml milk
- 60ml vegetable oil
- 1 tsp vanilla extract
- 75g fresh strawberries, diced
- 75g fresh rhubarb, diced

Chapter 03: Muffins

Cranberry Pistachio Muffins

Prep: 15 Min | Cook: 15 Min | Serves: 6 mufins

Ingredient:

- 175g self-raising flour
- 75g granulated sugar
- 1/4 tsp salt
- 1 large egg
- 125ml milk
- 60ml vegetable oil
- 1 tsp vanilla extract
- 75g dried cranberries
- 50g shelled pistachios, chopped

Instruction:

1. In a mixing bowl, whisk together the self-raising flour, granulated sugar, and salt.
2. In a separate bowl, beat the egg, then add the milk, vegetable oil, and vanilla extract. Mix well.
3. Pour the wet ingredients into the dry ingredients and stir until just combined.
4. Gently fold in the dried cranberries and chopped pistachios.
5. Line the air fryer basket with silicone liners or use silicone muffin cups.
6. Spoon the muffin batter into the lined air fryer basket, filling each cup about 2/3 full.
7. Place the basket in the air fryer. Set the temperature to 180°C and the cooking time to 15 minutes.
8. Once the cooking time is up, carefully remove the muffins from the air fryer and let them cool slightly. Serve the **Cranberry Pistachio Muffins** and enjoy!

Blueberry Cheesecake Muffins

Prep: 20 Min | Cook: 15 Min | Serves: 12 muffins

Ingredient:

- 200g self-raising flour
- 100g caster sugar
- 1/2 tsp baking powder
- 1/4 tsp salt
- 2 large eggs
- 180ml milk
- 80ml vegetable oil
- 1 tsp vanilla extract
- 100g fresh blueberries
- 150g cream cheese, softened
- 50g icing sugar
- 1 tsp lemon zest (optional)

Instruction:

1. Combine flour, caster sugar, baking powder, and salt. Whisk eggs, milk, vegetable oil, and vanilla extract. Mix wet and dry ingredients until just combined.
2. Gently fold in the fresh blueberries. Line a muffin pan with paper liners or grease the muffin cups. Divide the muffin batter evenly among the cups, filling each about 2/3 full.
3. Mix softened cream cheese and icing sugar until smooth. Place a dollop of cream cheese mixture on top of each muffin.
4. Use a toothpick or skewer to swirl the cream cheese mixture into the muffin batter.
5. Place the muffin pan into the air fryer basket, ensuring there is enough space around it for air circulation.
6. Cook the muffins in the air fryer at 180°C for approximately 15 minutes or until a toothpick inserted into the center comes out clean.
7. Once cooked, remove the muffins from the air fryer and let them cool in the pan for a few minutes. Transfer the **Blueberry Cheesecake Muffins** to a wire rack to cool completely.

Mocha Chocolate Chip Muffins

Prep: 15 Min | Cook: 15 Min | Serves: 6 muffins

Ingredient:

- 175g self-raising flour
- 50g granulated sugar
- 25g cocoa powder
- 1 tsp instant coffee granules
- 1/4 tsp salt
- 1 large egg
- 125ml milk
- 60ml vegetable oil
- 1 tsp vanilla extract
- 50g chocolate chips

Instruction:

1. In a mixing bowl, whisk together the self-raising flour, granulated sugar, cocoa powder, instant coffee granules, and salt.
2. In a separate bowl, beat the egg, then add the milk, vegetable oil, and vanilla extract. Mix well.
3. Pour the wet ingredients into the dry ingredients and stir until just combined.
4. Gently fold in the chocolate chips.
5. Line the air fryer basket with silicone liners or use silicone muffin cups.
6. Spoon the muffin batter into the lined air fryer basket, filling each cup about 2/3 full.
7. Place the basket in the air fryer. Set the temperature to 180°C and the cooking time to 15 minutes.
8. Once the cooking time is up, carefully remove the muffins from the air fryer and let them cool slightly. Serve the **Mocha Chocolate Chip Muffins** and enjoy!

Instruction:

1. In a mixing bowl, whisk together the self-raising flour, granulated sugar, and salt.
2. In a separate bowl, beat the egg, then add the milk, vegetable oil, and vanilla extract. Mix well.
3. Pour the wet ingredients into the dry ingredients and stir until just combined.
4. Gently fold in the chopped cherries and chocolate chips.
5. Line the air fryer basket with silicone liners or use silicone muffin cups.
6. Spoon the muffin batter into the lined air fryer basket, filling each cup about 2/3 full.
7. Place the basket in the air fryer. Set the temperature to 180°C and the cooking time to 15 minutes.
8. Once the cooking time is up, carefully remove the muffins from the air fryer and let them cool slightly. Serve the **Cherry Chocolate Chip Muffins** and enjoy!

Cherry Chocolate Chip Muffins

Prep: 15 Min | Cook: 15 Min | Serves: 6 muffins

Ingredient:

- 175g self-raising flour
- 75g granulated sugar
- 1/4 tsp salt
- 1 large egg
- 125ml milk
- 60ml vegetable oil
- 1 tsp vanilla extract
- 75g fresh cherries, pitted and chopped
- 50g chocolate chips

Sugar Cookies

Prep: 15 Min | Cook: 10 Min | Serves: 24 cookies

Ingredient:

- 200g unsalted butter, softened
- 200g caster sugar
- 2 large eggs
- 1 teaspoon vanilla extract
- 400g plain flour
- 1 teaspoon baking powder
- Pinch of salt
- Icing sugar, for decoration

Instruction:

1. In a mixing bowl, cream together the softened butter and caster sugar until light and fluffy.
2. Add the eggs, one at a time, beating well after each addition. Stir in the vanilla extract.
3. In a separate bowl, sift together the plain flour, baking powder, and salt.
4. Gradually add the dry ingredients to the butter mixture, stirring until the dough comes together. You may need to use your hands to fully incorporate the flour.
5. Divide the dough in half and form each portion into a log about 5cm in diameter. Wrap the logs in cling film and refrigerate for at least 1 hour.
6. Slice the cookie dough logs into rounds, about 1cm thick.
7. Place the cookie rounds in a single layer in the air fryer basket, leaving some space between each cookie.
8. Cook the cookies in the air fryer for 8-10 minutes, until the edges are lightly golden.
9. Remove the cookies from the air fryer and let them cool on a wire rack. Once cooled, dust the **Sugar Cookies** with icing sugar for decoration.

Instruction:

1. n a mixing bowl, cream together the softened butter and icing sugar until light and fluffy.
2. Add the ground pecans, vanilla extract, and a pinch of salt to the mixture. Mix well.
3. Gradually add the plain flour, stirring until a crumbly dough forms.
4. Shape the dough into a ball, wrap it in cling film, and refrigerate for at least 1 hour. After chilling, remove the dough from the refrigerator..
5. Divide the dough into equal portions and roll each portion into a log shape, about 2cm in diameter.
6. Cut the logs into 1.5cm thick slices and place them in the air fryer basket.
7. Cook the cookies in the air fryer at 160°C for approximately 12 minutes or until they turn golden brown.
8. Once cooked, remove the cookies from the air fryer and allow them to cool on a wire rack. Serve and enjoy your homemade **Pecan Sandies!**

Pecan Sandies

Prep: 15 Min | Cook: 12 Min | Serves: 12 cookies

Ingredient:

- 200g plain flour
- 100g unsalted butter, softened
- 75g icing sugar
- 50g ground pecans
- 1 tsp vanilla extract
- Pinch of salt

Chapter 04: Cookies

Linzer Cookies

Prep: 30 Min | Cook: 10 Min | Serves: 24 cookies

Ingredient:

- 200g plain flour
- 100g unsalted butter, softened
- 75g icing sugar
- 1 large egg yolk
- 1 tsp vanilla extract
- 100g raspberry jam (or any other preferred jam)
- Icing sugar, for dusting

Instruction:

1. In a mixing bowl, cream together the softened butter and caster sugar until light and fluffy. Add the egg yolk and vanilla extract to the bowl and mix until well combined. Gradually add the plain flour and ground almonds to the mixture, mixing until a dough forms.
2. Divide the dough into two portions and shape each portion into a disc. Wrap them in cling film and refrigerate for 1 hour.
3. Remove the chilled dough from the refrigerator and roll it out on a lightly floured surface to a thickness of about 5mm. Use a round cookie cutter to cut out 24 cookies from the rolled dough.
4. Place half of the cookies on the air fryer basket. Spoon a small amount of raspberry jam onto each cookie and spread it slightly, leaving a border around the edges.
5. Use a smaller cookie cutter to cut out the centers from the remaining cookies. These will be the tops of the Linzer cookies.
6. Place the cut-out cookies on top of the jam-covered cookies in the air fryer basket. Cook the cookies in the air fryer at 160°C for 10 minutes or until lightly golden.
7. Once cooked, carefully remove the cookies from the air fryer and let them cool on a wire rack. Dust the cookies with icing sugar before serving. Enjoy the delightful **Linzer Cookies** with a cup of tea or coffee.

Instruction:

1. In a saucepan, melt the butter and golden syrup (or honey) over low heat until well combined. Remove from heat and set aside.
2. In a large mixing bowl, combine the rolled oats, desiccated coconut, plain flour, and granulated sugar.
3. Dissolve the baking soda in the boiling water, then add it to the melted butter mixture.
4. Pour the wet ingredients into the dry ingredients and mix until well combined.
5. Line the air fryer basket with silicone liners or use silicone baking mats.
6. Take spoonfuls of the mixture and roll them into balls, then flatten them slightly to form biscuits. Place them on the lined air fryer basket, leaving space between each biscuit.
7. Place the basket in the air fryer. Set the temperature to 180°C and the cooking time to 10 minutes.
8. Once the cooking time is up, carefully remove the biscuits from the air fryer and let them cool on a wire rack. Serve and enjoy your homemade **Anzac Biscuits!**

Anzac Biscuits

Prep: 15 Min | Cook: 10 Min | Serves: 12 biscuits

Ingredient:

- 100g unsalted butter
- 100g golden syrup or honey
- 100g rolled oats
- 100g desiccated coconut
- 100g plain flour
- 100g granulated sugar
- 1/2 tsp baking soda
- 2 tbsp boiling water

Chapter 04: Cookies

Funfetti Cookies

Prep: 10 Min | Cook: 10 Min | Serves: 12 cookies

Ingredient:

- 150g unsalted butter, softened
- 150g granulated sugar
- 1 large egg
- 1 tsp vanilla extract
- 300g plain flour
- 1 tsp baking powder
- 1/4 tsp salt
- 50g rainbow sprinkles

Instruction:

1. In a mixing bowl, cream together the softened butter and granulated sugar until light and fluffy.
2. Beat in the egg and vanilla extract until well combined.
3. In a separate bowl, whisk together the plain flour, baking powder, and salt.
4. Gradually add the dry ingredients to the butter mixture, mixing until a dough forms.
5. Gently fold in the rainbow sprinkles, ensuring they are evenly distributed throughout the dough.
6. Line the air fryer basket with silicone liners or use silicone baking mats.
7. Take spoonfuls of the dough and roll them into balls, then flatten them slightly to form cookies. Place them on the lined air fryer basket, leaving space between each cookie.
8. Place the basket in the air fryer. Set the temperature to 180°C and the cooking time to 10 minutes.
9. Once the cooking time is up, carefully remove the cookies from the air fryer and let them cool on a wire rack. Serve and enjoy your homemade **Funfetti Cookies!**

Instruction:

1. In a mixing bowl, cream together the softened butter and light brown sugar until light and fluffy.
2. Beat in the egg and vanilla extract until well combined.
3. In a separate bowl, whisk together the plain flour, baking powder, and salt.
4. Gradually add the dry ingredients to the butter mixture, mixing until a dough forms.
5. Gently fold in the trail mix, ensuring it is evenly distributed throughout the dough.
6. Line the air fryer basket with silicone liners or use silicone baking mats.
7. Take spoonfuls of the dough and roll them into balls, then flatten them slightly to form cookies. Place them on the lined air fryer basket, leaving space between each cookie.
8. Place the basket in the air fryer. Set the temperature to 180°C and the cooking time to 10 minutes.
9. Once the cooking time is up, carefully remove the cookies from the air fryer and let them cool on a wire rack. Serve and enjoy your homemade **Trail Mix Cookies!**

Trail Mix Cookies

Prep: 15 Min | Cook: 10 Min | Serves: 12 muffins

Ingredient:

- 100g unsalted butter, softened
- 100g light brown sugar
- 1 large egg
- 1 tsp vanilla extract
- 150g plain flour
- 1/2 tsp baking powder
- 1/4 tsp salt
- 100g trail mix (a mix of nuts, dried fruits, and chocolate chips)

Shortbread Cookies

Prep: 10 Min | Cook: 12 Min | Serves: 12 cookies

Ingredient:

- 200g unsalted butter, softened
- 100g caster sugar
- 300g plain flour
- A pinch of salt

Instruction:

1. In a mixing bowl, cream together the softened butter and caster sugar until light and fluffy.
2. In a separate bowl, whisk together the plain flour and a pinch of salt.
3. Gradually add the dry ingredients to the butter mixture, mixing until a dough forms.
4. Shape the dough into a ball, wrap it in cling film, and refrigerate for at least 30 minutes.
5. After chilling, remove the dough from the refrigerator and roll it out on a lightly floured surface to a thickness of about 1 cm.
6. Use a cookie cutter to cut out individual cookies and place them on the air fryer basket lined with silicone liners or use silicone baking mats.
7. Place the basket in the air fryer. Set the temperature to 160°C and the cooking time to 12 minutes.
8. Once the cooking time is up, carefully remove the cookies from the air fryer and let them cool on a wire rack. Serve and enjoy your homemade **Shortbread Cookies!**

Instruction:

1. In a mixing bowl, cream together the softened butter and light brown sugar until light and fluffy. Add the egg and golden syrup to the butter mixture, and mix until well combined.
2. In a separate bowl, sift together the plain flour, baking powder, ground ginger, and ground cinnamon.
3. Gradually add the dry ingredients to the butter mixture, stirring until the dough comes together. You may need to use your hands to fully incorporate the flour.
4. Form the dough into a ball, wrap it in cling film, and refrigerate for at least 1 hour.
5. Roll out the dough on a lightly floured surface to a thickness of about 0.5cm.
6. Use cookie cutters to cut out gingerbread shapes from the rolled dough.
7. Place the gingerbread shapes in a single layer in the air fryer basket, leaving some space between each cookie.
8. Cook the cookies in the air fryer for 8-10 minutes, until the edges are lightly golden.
9. Remove the cookies from the air fryer and let them cool on a wire rack. Once cooled, decorate the **Gingerbread Cookies** with icing sugar, if desired.

Gingerbread Cookies

Prep: 15 Min | Cook: 10 Min | Serves: 24 cookies

Ingredient:

- 150g unsalted butter, softened
- 150g light brown sugar
- 1 large egg
- 4 tablespoons golden syrup
- 350g plain flour
- 1 teaspoon baking powder
- 1 teaspoon ground ginger
- 1 teaspoon ground cinnamon
- Icing sugar, for decoration

Chapter 04: Cookies

Maple Pecan Cookies

Prep: 15 Min | Cook: 10 Min | Serves: 12 cookies

Ingredient:

- 100g unsalted butter, softened
- 100g light brown sugar
- 1 large egg
- 2 tbsp maple syrup
- 200g plain flour
- 1/2 tsp baking powder
- 1/4 tsp salt
- 100g pecans, chopped

Instruction:

1. In a mixing bowl, cream together the softened butter and light brown sugar until light and fluffy.
2. Beat in the egg and maple syrup until well combined.
3. In a separate bowl, whisk together the plain flour, baking powder, and salt.
4. Gradually add the dry ingredients to the butter mixture, mixing until a dough forms.
5. Gently fold in the chopped pecans, ensuring they are evenly distributed throughout the dough.
6. Line the air fryer basket with silicone liners or use silicone baking mats.
7. Take spoonfuls of the dough and roll them into balls, then flatten them slightly to form cookies. Place them on the lined air fryer basket, leaving space between each cookie.
8. Place the basket in the air fryer. Set the temperature to 180°C and the cooking time to 10 minutes.
9. Once the cooking time is up, carefully remove the cookies from the air fryer and let them cool on a wire rack. Serve and enjoy your homemade **Maple Pecan Cookies!**

Maple Bacon Cookies

Prep: 15 Min | Cook: 10 Min | Serves: 12 cookies

Ingredient:

- 100g unsalted butter, softened
- 100g light brown sugar
- 1 egg
- 2 tbsp maple syrup
- 200g plain flour
- 1/2 tsp baking powder
- 1/4 tsp salt
- 100g cooked bacon, chopped into small pieces
- 50g chopped pecans (optional)

Instruction:

1. In a mixing bowl, cream together the softened butter and brown sugar until light and fluffy.
2. Add the egg and maple syrup to the bowl and mix until well combined.
3. In a separate bowl, whisk together the flour, baking powder, and salt.
4. Gradually add the dry ingredients to the wet ingredients, mixing until a dough forms.
5. Fold in the chopped bacon and chopped pecans (if using) into the dough.
6. Divide the dough into 12 equal portions and shape them into balls. Flatten the balls slightly.
7. Place the cookie dough portions into the air fryer basket, leaving space between each cookie.
8. Cook the cookies in the air fryer at 180°C for 10 minutes or until golden brown.
9. Once cooked, carefully remove the cookies from the air fryer and let them cool on a wire rack.
10. Enjoy the delicious **Maple Bacon Cookies** with a cup of tea or coffee.

Toffee Pecan Cookies

Prep: 20 Min | Cook: 10 Min | Serves: 24 cookies

Ingredient:

- 200g unsalted butter, softened
- 150g light brown sugar
- 100g caster sugar
- 2 large eggs
- 1 tsp vanilla extract
- 300g self-raising flour
- 100g toffee pieces
- 100g chopped pecans

Instruction:

1. In a mixing bowl, cream together the softened butter, light brown sugar, and caster sugar until light and fluffy.
2. Beat in the eggs, one at a time, followed by the vanilla extract.
3. Gradually add the self-raising flour to the mixture, mixing well after each addition, until a dough forms.
4. Fold in the toffee pieces and chopped pecans until evenly distributed throughout the dough.
5. Line the air fryer basket with parchment paper or use a silicone baking mat.
6. Scoop tablespoon-sized portions of the cookie dough onto the lined air fryer basket, spacing them apart to allow for spreading during baking.
7. Place the cookies in the air fryer basket, ensuring there is enough space around them for air circulation.
8. Cook the cookies in the air fryer at 180°C for 10 minutes per batch or until they turn golden brown around the edges.
9. Once cooked, remove the cookies from the air fryer and let them cool on a wire rack.
10. Repeat the process with the remaining **Toffee Pecan Cookies** dough until all the cookies are baked.

Coconut Lime Cookies

Prep: 15 Min | Cook: 10 Min | Serves: 12 cookies

Ingredient:

- 100g unsalted butter, softened
- 100g caster sugar
- 1 large egg
- Zest of 1 lime
- 1 tbsp lime juice
- 150g plain flour
- 50g desiccated coconut
- 1/2 tsp baking powder
- A pinch of salt

Instruction:

1. In a mixing bowl, cream together the softened butter and caster sugar until light and fluffy.
2. Beat in the egg, lime zest, and lime juice until well combined.
3. In a separate bowl, whisk together the plain flour, desiccated coconut, baking powder, and salt.
4. Gradually add the dry ingredients to the butter mixture, mixing until a dough forms.
5. Line the air fryer basket with silicone liners or use silicone baking mats.
6. Take spoonfuls of the dough and roll them into balls, then flatten them slightly to form cookies. Place them on the lined air fryer basket, leaving space between each cookie.
7. Place the basket in the air fryer. Set the temperature to 180°C and the cooking time to 10 minutes.
8. Once the cooking time is up, carefully remove the cookies from the air fryer and let them cool on a wire rack. Serve and enjoy your homemade **Coconut Lime Cookies!**

Macadamia Nut Cookies

Prep: 15 Min | Cook: 10 Min | Serves: 15 cookies

Ingredient:

- 150g unsalted butter, softened
- 150g caster sugar
- 1 large egg
- 1 tsp vanilla extract
- 225g self-raising flour
- 100g macadamia nuts, roughly chopped

Instruction:

1. In a mixing bowl, cream together the softened butter and caster sugar until light and fluffy.
2. Add the egg and vanilla extract to the butter mixture and mix until well combined.
3. Sift in the self-raising flour and mix until a dough forms.
4. Add the roughly chopped macadamia nuts to the dough. Mix until they are evenly distributed.
5. Line the air fryer basket with parchment paper or a silicone baking mat.
6. Take spoonfuls of the cookie dough and shape them into balls. Place the cookie dough balls onto the lined air fryer basket, leaving space between them for spreading.
7. Place the basket in the air fryer. Set the air fryer temperature to 180°C and the cooking time to 10 minutes.
8. Once the cookies are cooked, carefully remove them from the air fryer and allow them to cool on a wire rack. Serve and enjoy the delicious **Macadamia Nut Cookies!**

Peanut Butter Cookies

Prep: 15 Min | Cook: 10 Min | Serves: 12 cookies

Ingredient:

- 100g unsalted butter, softened
- 100g caster sugar
- 100g light brown sugar
- 1 large egg
- 125g smooth peanut butter
- 200g plain flour
- 1/2 tsp baking powder
- 1/4 tsp salt

Instruction:

1. In a mixing bowl, cream together the softened butter, caster sugar, and light brown sugar until light and fluffy.
2. Beat in the egg and smooth peanut butter until well combined.
3. In a separate bowl, whisk together the plain flour, baking powder, and salt.
4. Gradually add the dry ingredients to the butter mixture, mixing until a dough forms.
5. Line the air fryer basket with silicone liners or use silicone baking mats.
6. Take spoonfuls of the dough and roll them into balls, then flatten them slightly to form cookies. Place them on the lined air fryer basket, leaving space between each cookie.
7. Place the basket in the air fryer. Set the temperature to 180°C and the cooking time to 10 minutes.
8. Once the cooking time is up, carefully remove the cookies from the air fryer and let them cool on a wire rack. Serve and enjoy your homemade **Peanut Butter Cookies!**

Chapter 04: Cookies

Almond Butter Cookies

Prep: 15 Min | Cook: 10 Min | Serves: 12 cookies

Ingredient:

- 100g unsalted butter, softened
- 100g caster sugar
- 1 large egg
- 125g almond butter
- 200g plain flour
- 1/2 tsp baking powder
- 1/4 tsp salt

Instruction:

1. In a mixing bowl, cream together the softened butter and caster sugar until light and fluffy.
2. Beat in the egg and almond butter until well combined.
3. In a separate bowl, whisk together the plain flour, baking powder, and salt.
4. Gradually add the dry ingredients to the butter mixture, mixing until a dough forms.
5. Line the air fryer basket with silicone liners or use silicone baking mats.
6. Take spoonfuls of the dough and roll them into balls, then flatten them slightly to form cookies. Place them on the lined air fryer basket, leaving space between each cookie.
7. Place the basket in the air fryer. Set the temperature to 180°C and the cooking time to 10 minutes.
8. Once the cooking time is up, carefully remove the cookies from the air fryer and let them cool on a wire rack. Serve and enjoy your homemade **Almond Butter Cookies!**

Bourbon Pecan Cookies

Prep: 15 Min | Cook: 10 Min | Serves: 12 cookies

Ingredient:

- 100g unsalted butter, softened
- 75g light brown sugar
- 1 egg
- 1 tsp vanilla extract
- 1 tbsp bourbon whiskey
- 175g plain flour
- 1/2 tsp baking powder
- 1/4 tsp salt
- 50g pecans, chopped

Instruction:

1. In a mixing bowl, cream together the softened butter and light brown sugar until light and fluffy.
2. Add the egg, vanilla extract, and bourbon whiskey to the bowl and mix until well combined.
3. In a separate bowl, whisk together the plain flour, baking powder, and salt.
4. Gradually add the dry ingredients to the wet ingredients, mixing until a dough forms.
5. Fold in the chopped pecans into the dough.
6. Divide the dough into 12 equal portions and shape them into balls. Flatten the balls slightly.
7. Place the cookie dough portions into the air fryer basket, leaving space between each cookie.
8. Cook the cookies in the air fryer at 180°C for 10 minutes or until golden brown.
9. Once cooked, carefully remove the cookies from the air fryer and let them cool on a wire rack.
10. Enjoy the delicious **Bourbon Pecan Cookies** with a cup of tea or coffee.

Chapter 04: Cookies

Apple Cinnamon Cookies

Prep: 20 Min | Cook: 12 Min | Serves: 12 cookies

Ingredient:

- 100g unsalted butter, softened
- 100g light brown sugar
- 1 large egg
- 1 tsp vanilla extract
- 150g plain flour
- 1/2 tsp baking powder
- 1/2 tsp ground cinnamon
- 1 medium-sized apple, peeled, cored, and finely diced
- 50g rolled oats

Instruction:

1. In a mixing bowl, cream together the softened butter and light brown sugar until light and fluffy.
2. Beat in the egg and vanilla extract until well combined.
3. In a separate bowl, whisk together the plain flour, baking powder, and ground cinnamon.
4. Gradually add the dry ingredients to the butter mixture, mixing until a dough forms.
5. Fold in the finely diced apple and rolled oats until evenly distributed throughout the dough.
6. Line the air fryer basket with silicone liners or use silicone baking mats.
7. Take spoonfuls of the dough and roll them into balls, then flatten them slightly to form cookies. Place them on the lined air fryer basket, leaving space between each cookie.
8. Place the basket in the air fryer. Set the temperature to 180°C and the cooking time to 12 minutes.
9. Once the cooking time is up, carefully remove the cookies from the air fryer and let them cool on a wire rack. Serve and enjoy your homemade **Apple Cinnamon Cookies!**

Mocha Hazelnut Cookies

Prep: 15 Min | Cook: 10 Min | Serves: 12 cookies

Ingredient:

- 100g unsalted butter, softened
- 100g light brown sugar
- 1 egg
- 1 tsp instant coffee granules
- 1 tsp hot water
- 200g plain flour
- 1/2 tsp baking powder
- 1/4 tsp salt
- 50g chopped hazelnuts
- 50g dark chocolate chips

Instruction:

1. In a small bowl, dissolve the instant coffee granules in hot water and set aside to cool.
2. In a mixing bowl, cream together the softened butter and brown sugar until light and fluffy.
3. Add the egg to the bowl and mix until well combined.
4. Stir in the cooled coffee mixture.
5. In a separate bowl, whisk together the flour, baking powder, and salt.
6. Gradually add the dry ingredients to the wet ingredients, mixing until a dough forms.
7. Fold in the chopped hazelnuts and dark chocolate chips into the dough.
8. Divide the dough into 12 equal portions and shape them into balls. Flatten the balls slightly.
9. Place the cookie dough portions into the air fryer basket, leaving space between each cookie.
10. Cook the cookies in the air fryer at 180°C for 10 minutes or until golden brown.
11. Once cooked, carefully remove the cookies from the air fryer and let them cool on a wire rack.
12. Enjoy the delicious **Mocha Hazelnut Cookies** with a cup of tea or coffee.

Chapter 04: Cookies

Fig and Walnut Biscuits

Prep: 20 Min | Cook: 10 Min | Serves: 12 cookies

Ingredient:

- 100g unsalted butter, softened
- 80g caster sugar
- 1 large egg
- 200g plain flour
- 1/2 tsp baking powder
- 1/4 tsp salt
- 100g dried figs, finely chopped
- 50g walnuts, finely chopped

Instruction:

1. In a mixing bowl, cream together the softened butter and caster sugar until light and fluffy.
2. Beat in the egg until well combined.
3. In a separate bowl, whisk together the plain flour, baking powder, and salt.
4. Gradually add the dry ingredients to the butter mixture, mixing until a dough forms.
5. Fold in the finely chopped dried figs and walnuts until evenly distributed throughout the dough.
6. Line the air fryer basket with silicone liners or use silicone baking mats.
7. Take spoonfuls of the dough and roll them into balls, then flatten them slightly to form biscuits (cookies). Place them on the lined air fryer basket, leaving space between each biscuit.
8. Place the basket in the air fryer. Set the temperature to 180°C and the cooking time to 10 minutes.
9. Once the cooking time is up, carefully remove the biscuits from the air fryer and let them cool on a wire rack. Serve and enjoy your homemade **Fig and Walnut Biscuits!**

Apricot Coconut Cookies

Prep: 15 Min | Cook: 10 Min | Serves: 12 cookies

Ingredient:

- 100g unsalted butter, softened
- 100g caster sugar
- 1 egg
- 1 tsp vanilla extract
- 150g self-raising flour
- 50g desiccated coconut
- 50g dried apricots, finely chopped
- 25g chopped almonds (optional)

Instruction:

1. In a mixing bowl, cream together the softened butter and caster sugar until light and fluffy.
2. Add the egg and vanilla extract to the bowl and mix until well combined.
3. In a separate bowl, whisk together the self-raising flour and desiccated coconut.
4. Gradually add the dry ingredients to the wet ingredients, mixing until a dough forms.
5. Fold in the dried apricots and chopped almonds (if using) into the dough.
6. Divide the dough into 12 equal portions and shape them into balls. Flatten the balls slightly.
7. Place the cookie dough portions into the air fryer basket, leaving space between each cookie.
8. Cook the cookies in the air fryer at 180°C for 10 minutes or until golden brown.
9. Once cooked, carefully remove the cookies from the air fryer and let them cool on a wire rack.
10. Enjoy the delicious **Apricot Coconut Cookies** with a cup of tea or coffee.

Double Chocolate Cookies

Prep: 20 Min | Cook: 10 Min | Serves: 12 cookies

Ingredient:

- 100g unsalted butter, softened
- 100g caster sugar
- 80g light brown sugar
- 1 large egg
- 1 tsp vanilla extract
- 175g plain flour
- 25g cocoa powder
- 1/2 tsp baking powder
- 1/4 tsp salt
- 100g chocolate chips (dark or milk, according to preference)

Instruction:

1. In a mixing bowl, cream together the softened butter, caster sugar, and light brown sugar until light and fluffy.
2. Beat in the egg and vanilla extract until well combined.
3. In a separate bowl, whisk together the plain flour, cocoa powder, baking powder, and salt.
4. Gradually add the dry ingredients to the butter mixture, mixing until a dough forms.
5. Fold in the chocolate chips until evenly distributed throughout the dough.
6. Line the air fryer basket with silicone liners or use silicone baking mats.
7. Take spoonfuls of the dough and roll them into balls, then flatten them slightly to form cookies. Place them on the lined air fryer basket, leaving space between each cookie.
8. Place the basket in the air fryer. Set the temperature to 180°C and the cooking time to 10 minutes.
9. Once the cooking time is up, carefully remove the cookies from the air fryer and let them cool on a wire rack. Serve and enjoy your homemade **Double Chocolate Cookies!**

Instruction:

1. In a mixing bowl, cream together the softened butter and caster sugar until light and fluffy.
2. Add the lemon zest and lemon juice to the bowl and mix until well combined.
3. Gradually add the plain flour to the mixture, mixing until a dough forms.
4. Shape the dough into a log, approximately 5cm in diameter.
5. Wrap the dough log in cling film and refrigerate for 1 hour.
6. Remove the chilled dough from the refrigerator and slice it into 12 equal rounds.
7. Place the shortbread rounds into the air fryer basket, leaving space between each cookie.
8. Cook the cookies in the air fryer at 160°C for 12 minutes or until the edges are lightly golden.
9. Once cooked, carefully remove the cookies from the air fryer and let them cool on a wire rack.
10. Enjoy the delightful **Lemon Shortbread Cookies** with a cup of tea or coffee.

Lemon Shortbread Cookies

Prep: 20 Min | Cook: 12 Min | Serves: 12 cookies

Ingredient:

- 150g unsalted butter, softened
- 75g caster sugar
- 1 lemon (zest only)
- 225g plain flour
- 1 tbsp lemon juice (freshly squeezed)

Cranberry Orange Cookies

Prep: 20 Min | Cook: 10 Min | Serves: 12 cookies

Ingredient:

- 100g unsalted butter, softened
- 100g caster sugar
- 1 large egg
- 1 tsp vanilla extract
- Zest of 1 orange
- 200g plain flour
- 1/2 tsp baking powder
- 1/4 tsp salt
- 100g dried cranberries

Instruction:

1. In a mixing bowl, cream together the softened butter and caster sugar until light and fluffy.
2. Beat in the egg, vanilla extract, and orange zest until well combined.
3. In a separate bowl, whisk together the plain flour, baking powder, and salt.
4. Gradually add the dry ingredients to the butter mixture, mixing until a dough forms.
5. Fold in the dried cranberries until evenly distributed throughout the dough.
6. Line the air fryer basket with silicone liners or use silicone baking mats.
7. Take spoonfuls of the dough and roll them into balls, then flatten them slightly to form cookies. Place them on the lined air fryer basket, leaving space between each cookie.
8. Place the basket in the air fryer. Set the temperature to 180°C and the cooking time to 10 minutes.
9. Once the cooking time is up, carefully remove the cookies from the air fryer and let them cool on a wire rack. Serve and enjoy your homemade **Cranberry Orange Cookies!**

Espresso Walnut Biscuits

Prep: 20 Min | Cook: 10 Min | Serves: 12 biscuits

Ingredient:

- 100g unsalted butter, softened
- 75g caster sugar
- 1 tsp instant espresso powder
- 1 tsp hot water
- 175g plain flour
- 50g walnuts, finely chopped

Instruction:

1. In a small bowl, dissolve the instant espresso powder in hot water and set aside to cool.
2. In a mixing bowl, cream together the softened butter and caster sugar until light and fluffy.
3. Add the cooled espresso mixture to the bowl and mix until well combined.
4. Gradually add the plain flour to the mixture, mixing until a dough forms.
5. Fold in the finely chopped walnuts into the dough.
6. Divide the dough into 12 equal portions and shape them into small round biscuits.
7. Place the biscuits into the air fryer basket, leaving space between each biscuit.
8. Cook the biscuits in the air fryer at 180°C for 10 minutes or until lightly golden.
9. Once cooked, carefully remove the biscuits from the air fryer and let them cool on a wire rack.
10. Enjoy the delightful **Espresso Walnut Biscuits** with a cup of tea or coffee.

Chapter 04: Cookies

Chocolate Crinkle Cookies

Prep: 20 Min | Cook: 10 Min | Serves: 12 cookies

Ingredient:

- 100g unsalted butter, melted
- 200g caster sugar
- 2 large eggs
- 1 tsp vanilla extract
- 200g plain flour
- 50g cocoa powder
- 2 tsp baking powder
- 1/4 tsp salt
- 100g icing sugar, for coating

Instruction:

1. In a mixing bowl, whisk together the melted butter and caster sugar until well combined.
2. Add the eggs and vanilla extract to the bowl, and whisk until smooth.
3. In a separate bowl, whisk together the plain flour, cocoa powder, baking powder, and salt.
4. Gradually add the dry ingredients to the wet ingredients, stirring until a thick dough forms.
5. Cover the dough with cling film and refrigerate for at least 1 hour to firm up.
6. Line the air fryer basket with silicone liners or use silicone baking mats.
7. Take spoonfuls of the chilled dough and roll them into balls, about 3 cm in diameter.
8. Roll each dough ball in the icing sugar until evenly coated, then place them on the lined air fryer basket, leaving space between each cookie.
9. Place the basket in the air fryer. Set the temperature to 180°C and the cooking time to 10 minutes.
10. Once the cooking time is up, carefully remove the cookies from the air fryer and let them cool on a wire rack. Serve and enjoy your homemade **Chocolate Crinkle Cookies!**

Instruction:

1. In a mixing bowl, cream together the softened unsalted butter, granulated sugar, and vanilla extract until light and fluffy.
2. Add the plain flour, salt, and ground almonds to the bowl. Mix until the dough comes together.
3. Divide the dough into small portions and roll each portion into 2.5 cm balls.
4. Place the dough balls on a parchment-lined tray that fits in your air fryer.
5. Use your thumb or the back of a spoon to make an indentation in the center of each dough ball.
6. Fill each indentation with approximately 1/2 teaspoon of raspberry jam.
7. Place the tray of thumbprints in the air fryer and cook at 180°C for about 10 minutes, or until the edges are golden brown.
8. Remove the tray from the air fryer and let the thumbprints cool completely on a wire rack.
9. Once cooled, enjoy your delightful **Raspberry Jam Thumbprints** with a buttery and nutty flavor, complemented by the sweet and tangy raspberry jam filling!

Raspberry Jam Thumbprints

Prep: 15 Min | Cook: 10 Min | Serves: 24 cookies

Ingredient:

- 200g unsalted butter, softened
- 100g granulated sugar
- 1 teaspoon vanilla extract
- 250g plain flour
- 1/4 teaspoon salt
- 100g ground almonds
- Approximately 1/2 cup raspberry jam

Lemon Lavender Shortbread

Prep: 20 Min | Cook: 12 Min | Serves: 24 cookies

Ingredient:

- 200g unsalted butter, softened
- 100g caster sugar
- Zest of 1 lemon
- 1 tsp dried lavender flowers (culinary-grade)
- 300g plain flour
- 1/4 tsp salt

Instruction:

1. In a mixing bowl, cream together the softened butter and caster sugar until light and fluffy.
2. Add the lemon zest and dried lavender flowers to the bowl, and mix until well combined.
3. In a separate bowl, whisk together the plain flour and salt.
4. Gradually add the dry ingredients to the butter mixture, mixing until a crumbly dough forms.
5. Turn the dough out onto a clean surface and knead it gently until it comes together into a smooth ball.
6. Roll out the dough to a thickness of about 1 cm.
7. Using a cookie cutter or a sharp knife, cut the dough into desired shapes (rounds, squares, etc.).
8. Line the air fryer basket with silicone liners or use silicone baking mats.
9. Place the shaped shortbread cookies on the lined air fryer basket, leaving space between each cookie.
10. Place the basket in the air fryer. Set the temperature to 160°C and the cooking time to 12 minutes.
11. Once the cooking time is up, carefully remove the cookies from the air fryer and let them cool on a wire rack. Serve and enjoy your homemade **Lemon Lavender Shortbread!**

Instruction:

1. In a mixing bowl, cream together the softened butter and caster sugar until light and fluffy. Add the egg and vanilla extract to the butter mixture and mix until well combined.
2. In a separate bowl, whisk together the plain flour and salt. Gradually add the dry ingredients to the butter mixture, mixing well after each addition.
3. Line the air fryer basket with parchment paper or use a silicone baking mat. Scoop tablespoon-sized portions of the cookie dough onto the lined air fryer basket, spacing them apart to allow for slight spreading.
4. Gently press your thumb or the back of a spoon into the center of each cookie to create a small indentation.
5. Fill each indentation with a small amount (about 1/2 teaspoon) of raspberry jam.
6. Place the cookies in the air fryer basket, ensuring there is enough space around them for air circulation. Cook the cookies in the air fryer at 180°C for 10-12 minutes or until they are lightly golden on the edges. Once cooked, remove the **Raspberry Thumbprint Cookies** from the air fryer and let them cool on a wire rack.

Raspberry Thumbprint Cookies

Prep: 20 Min | Cook: 12 Min | Serves: 24 cookies

Ingredient:

- 200g unsalted butter, softened
- 150g caster sugar
- 1 large egg
- 1 tsp vanilla extract
- 250g plain flour
- 1/4 tsp salt
- 100g raspberry jam

Chapter 04: Cookies

Chapati

Prep: 20 Min | Cook: 6 Min | Serves: 6 chapatis

Ingredient:

- 250g whole wheat flour
- 1/2 teaspoon salt
- 150ml warm water (adjust as needed)
- 1 tablespoon vegetable oil, plus extra for brushing

Instruction:

1. In a mixing bowl, combine the whole wheat flour and salt. Gradually add the warm water to the flour mixture, mixing with your hands or a spoon, until a soft and pliable dough forms. Adjust the amount of water as needed.
2. Add the vegetable oil to the dough and knead it for a few minutes until smooth and elastic. Divide the dough into 6 equal portions and shape each portion into a ball.
3. On a lightly floured surface, roll out each ball into a thin, round chapati of approximately 15 cm in diameter.
4. Place a chapati in the air fryer basket and cook at 180°C for about 2-3 minutes, or until it puffs up and shows golden brown spots. Flip the chapati and cook for an additional 2-3 minutes on the other side.
5. Repeat the cooking process with the remaining chapatis. Once cooked, lightly brush each chapati with a little vegetable oil. Serve your delicious **Chapatis** warm and enjoy them as a versatile accompaniment to curries, stews, or as a wrap for fillings!

Flatbread

Prep: 15 Min | Cook: 6 Min | Serves: 6 flatbreads

Ingredient:

- 300g plain flour
- 2 teaspoons baking powder
- 1/2 teaspoon salt
- 200g natural yogurt
- 2 tablespoons olive oil
- Additional flour for dusting

Instruction:

1. In a mixing bowl, whisk together the plain flour, baking powder, and salt.
2. Add the natural yogurt and olive oil to the bowl. Mix until the ingredients come together to form a dough.
3. Transfer the dough onto a lightly floured surface and knead it for a few minutes until it becomes smooth and elastic.
4. Divide the dough into 6 equal portions and shape each portion into a ball.
5. Roll out each ball into a thin, round flatbread, approximately 0.5 cm thick.
6. Place the flatbreads in the air fryer basket, ensuring they are not overlapping.
7. Cook the flatbreads in the air fryer at 180°C for about 6 minutes, or until they are puffed up and lightly golden brown.
8. Remove the flatbreads from the air fryer and let them cool slightly on a wire rack.
9. Once cooled, serve your delicious **Flatbread** warm and enjoy it as a side to curries, soups, or dips!

Chapter 05: Breads

Naan Bread

Prep: 90 Min | Cook: 5 Min | Serves: 4 breads

Ingredient:

- 250g plain flour
- 1 tsp instant yeast
- 1 tsp sugar
- 1/2 tsp salt
- 1/4 tsp baking powder
- 2 tbsp plain yogurt
- 2 tbsp vegetable oil
- 120ml warm milk
- Butter or ghee, for brushing (optional)
- Fresh coriander leaves, for garnish (optional)

Instruction:

1. In a mixing bowl, combine the plain flour, instant yeast, sugar, salt, and baking powder.
2. Add the plain yogurt and vegetable oil to the bowl, and mix well. Gradually add the warm milk to the mixture, stirring until a soft dough forms.
3. Transfer the dough to a floured surface and knead for about 5-7 minutes until the dough is smooth and elastic.
4. Place the dough in a greased bowl, cover it with a clean kitchen towel, and let it rest in a warm place for about 1 hour or until it doubles in size. After the dough has risen, divide it into 4 equal-sized portions.
5. Take one portion of the dough and roll it out into an oval or round shape, about 0.5 cm thick.
6. Place the rolled naan bread in the air fryer at 180°C basket and cook for 4-5 minutes, or until it puffs up and turns golden brown. Flip it halfway through the cooking time. Repeat the process with the remaining dough portions.
7. Once cooked, remove the **Naan Bread** from the air fryer and brush them with melted butter or ghee, if desired. Garnish with fresh coriander leaves, if desired, and serve warm.

Instruction:

1. In a mixing bowl, combine the strong white bread flour, salt, and instant yeast.
2. Add the olive oil to the bowl and gradually pour in the warm water while mixing the ingredients with your hands or a spoon. Continue to mix until a soft and slightly sticky dough forms. Adjust the amount of water or flour as needed.
3. Transfer the dough onto a lightly floured surface and knead it for about 5 minutes until smooth and elastic. Divide the dough into 6 equal portions and shape each portion into a ball.
4. On a lightly floured surface, roll out each ball into a round pita bread of approximately 15 cm in diameter and 0.5 cm thick.
5. Place a pita bread in the air fryer basket and cook at 180°C for about 3 minutes, or until it puffs up and shows golden brown spots. Flip the pita bread and cook for an additional 2-3 minutes on the other side.
6. Repeat the cooking process with the remaining pita breads.
7. Once cooked, remove the pita breads from the air fryer and let them cool slightly on a wire rack. Serve your delicious **Pita Bread** warm and enjoy them with fillings, dips, or as a base for sandwiches!

Pita Bread

Prep: 20 Min | Cook: 6 Min | Serves: 6 breads

Ingredient:

- 300g strong white bread flour
- 1 teaspoon salt
- 1 teaspoon instant yeast
- 1 tablespoon olive oil
- 200ml warm water (adjust as needed)

Herb Knots

Prep: 10 Min | Cook: 10 Min | Serves: 12 knots

Ingredient:

- 350g strong white bread flour
- 1 teaspoon salt
- 1 teaspoon dried mixed herbs
- 1 teaspoon garlic powder
- 7g instant yeast
- 1 tablespoon olive oil
- 225ml warm water (adjust as needed)
- Additional olive oil for brushing
- Coarse sea salt for sprinkling

Instruction:

1. In a mixing bowl, combine the strong white bread flour, salt, dried mixed herbs, garlic powder, and instant yeast.
2. Add the olive oil to the bowl and gradually pour in the warm water while mixing the ingredients with your hands or a spoon. Continue to mix until a slightly sticky dough forms. Adjust the amount of water or flour as needed.
3. Transfer the dough onto a lightly floured surface and knead it for about 5 minutes until smooth and elastic. Divide the dough into 12 equal portions and shape each portion into a rope of approximately 15 cm in length.
4. Tie each rope into a knot, tucking the ends underneath. Place the knots in the air fryer basket, ensuring they are not touching.
5. Cook the herb knots in the air fryer at 180°C for about 10 minutes, or until they are golden brown.
6. Remove the herb knots from the air fryer and let them cool slightly on a wire rack.
7. While still warm, brush the herb knots with olive oil and sprinkle them with coarse sea salt. Serve your delicious **Herb Knots** warm and enjoy them as a flavorful side to soups, stews, or as a snack!

Instruction:

1. In a mixing bowl, combine the strong white bread flour, wholemeal bread flour, mixed seeds, salt, and instant yeast.
2. Add the olive oil to the bowl and gradually pour in the warm water while mixing the ingredients with your hands or a spoon.
3. Continue to mix until a slightly sticky dough forms. Adjust the amount of water or flour as needed.
4. Transfer the dough onto a lightly floured surface and knead it for about 10 minutes until smooth and elastic.
5. Shape the dough into a loaf by rolling it tightly from one end.
6. Place the shaped loaf in a greased or parchment-lined air fryer basket.
7. Place the basket with the seed bread in the air fryer and cook at 180°C for about 25 minutes, or until the bread is golden brown and sounds hollow when tapped on the bottom.
8. Remove the seed bread from the air fryer and let it cool on a wire rack before slicing.
9. Serve your delicious **Seed Bread** sliced and enjoy it as a hearty and flavorful accompaniment to soups, sandwiches, or with your favorite spreads!

Seed Bread

Prep: 15 Min | Cook: 25 Min | Serves: 1 loaf

Ingredient:

- 250g strong white bread flour
- 100g wholemeal bread flour
- 50g mixed seeds (such as sunflower seeds, pumpkin seeds, and sesame seeds)
- 1 teaspoon salt
- 1 teaspoon instant yeast
- 1 tablespoon olive oil
- 275ml warm water (adjust as needed)

Chapter 05: Breads

Onion Bread

Prep: 90 Min | Cook: 18 Min | Serves: 8 slices

Ingredient:

- 300g strong white bread flour
- 1 tsp instant yeast
- 1 tsp sugar
- 1/2 tsp salt
- 1 tbsp olive oil
- 180ml warm water
- 2 medium onions, thinly sliced
- 1 tbsp olive oil
- 1 tsp dried thyme
- 1/2 tsp salt
- Freshly ground black pepper, to taste

Instruction:

1. In a mixing bowl, combine the bread flour, instant yeast, sugar, and salt. Add the olive oil and warm water to the bowl, and mix until a soft dough forms.
2. Transfer the dough to a floured surface and knead for about 10 minutes until the dough is smooth and elastic. Let dough rise for 1 hour.
3. Add the thinly sliced onions and cook until caramelized, stirring occasionally. This process may take about 15-20 minutes. Once caramelized, remove the onions from the heat and set aside.
4. After the dough has risen, punch it down to release the air, and transfer it back to the floured surface. Roll out the dough into a rectangular shape, about 1 cm thick.
5. Spread the caramelized onions evenly over the surface of the dough, leaving a small border around the edges. Sprinkle the dried thyme, salt, and freshly ground black pepper over the onions.
6. Starting from one of the longer edges, tightly roll up the dough into a log shape. Place the rolled dough in the air fryer basket and cook for 15-18 minutes at 180°C, or until the bread is golden brown and cooked through.
7. Once cooked, carefully remove the **Onion bread** from the air fryer and let it cool slightly before slicing.

Instruction:

1. Cut the baguette into slices, about 2 cm thick.
2. In a small bowl, combine the softened butter, minced garlic, fresh parsley, and salt. Mix well until all ingredients are evenly incorporated.
3. Spread the garlic butter mixture onto one side of each bread slice.
4. Place the garlic bread slices into the air fryer basket, buttered side up, in a single layer. You may need to cook them in batches, depending on the size of your air fryer.
5. Cook the garlic bread in the air fryer at 180°C for about 4-5 minutes, or until the bread is golden brown and crispy.
6. Remove the garlic bread from the air fryer and let it cool slightly before serving.
7. Serve your delicious **Garlic Bread** warm and enjoy it as a tasty side to pasta dishes, soups, or as a snack!

Garlic Bread

Prep: 10 Min | Cook: 5 Min | Serves: 4

Ingredient:

- 1 large baguette (about 250g)
- 100g unsalted butter, softened
- 3 garlic cloves, minced
- 2 tablespoons fresh parsley, finely chopped
- 1/4 teaspoon salt

Chapter 05: Breads

Garlic Knots

Prep: 15 Min | Cook: 10 Min | Serves: 12 knots

Ingredient:

- 350g strong white bread flour
- 1 teaspoon salt
- 1 teaspoon dried parsley
- 1 teaspoon garlic powder
- 7g instant yeast
- 1 tablespoon olive oil
- 225ml warm water (adjust as needed)
- 50g unsalted butter, melted
- 2 garlic cloves, minced
- 2 tablespoons fresh parsley, finely chopped
- Coarse sea salt, for sprinkling

Instruction:

1. In a mixing bowl, combine the strong white bread flour, salt, dried parsley, garlic powder, and instant yeast.
2. Add the olive oil to the bowl and gradually pour in the warm water while mixing the ingredients with your hands or a spoon. Continue to mix until a slightly sticky dough forms. Adjust the amount of water or flour as needed.
3. Transfer the dough onto a lightly floured surface and knead it for about 5 minutes until smooth and elastic. Divide the dough into 12 equal portions and shape each portion into a rope of approximately 15 cm in length.
4. Tie each rope into a knot, tucking the ends underneath. Place the knots in the air fryer basket, ensuring they are not touching.
5. Cook the garlic knots in the air fryer at 180°C for about 10 minutes, or until they are golden brown.
6. While the knots are cooking, prepare the garlic topping. In a small bowl, mix together the melted butter, minced garlic, and fresh parsley.
7. Once the knots are cooked, remove them from the air fryer and imediately brush them with the garlic topping. Sprinkle the garlic knots with coarse sea salt. Serve your delicious **Garlic Knots** warm and enjoy them as a flavorful side to pasta dishes, soups, or as a snack!

Instruction:

1. n a mixing bowl, combine the strong white bread flour, salt, and instant yeast.
2. Gradually add the warm water to the flour mixture, mixing with your hands or a spoon, until a soft and slightly sticky dough forms. Adjust the amount of water or flour as needed.
3. Transfer the dough onto a lightly floured surface and knead it for about 10 minutes until smooth and elastic.
4. Shape the dough into a round loaf by folding the edges towards the center, rotating the dough as you go.
5. Grease the air fryer basket with olive oil and place the shaped loaf inside, seam side down.
6. Cook the bread in the air fryer at 180°C for about 20 minutes, or until it is golden brown and sounds hollow when tapped on the bottom.
7. Remove the rustic bread from the air fryer and let it cool on a wire rack before slicing.
8. Serve your delicious **Rustic Bread** sliced and enjoy it as a versatile accompaniment to soups, stews, or as a base for sandwiches!

Rustic Bread

Prep: 15 Min | Cook: 20 Min | Serves: 1 loaf

Ingredient:

- 500g strong white bread flour
- 10g salt
- 7g instant yeast
- 350ml warm water (adjust as needed)
- Olive oil, for greasing

Chapter 05: Breads

Potato Bread

Prep: 90 Min | Cook: 25 Min | Serves: 1 loaf

Ingredient:

- 400g strong white bread flour
- 100g mashed potatoes (cooled)
- 1 tsp instant yeast
- 1 tsp sugar
- 1 tsp salt
- 25g unsalted butter, softened
- 240ml warm water

Instruction:

1. In a mixing bowl, combine the bread flour, mashed potatoes, instant yeast, sugar, salt, softened butter, and warm water.
2. Mix the ingredients until a dough forms.
3. Transfer the dough to a floured surface and knead for about 10 minutes until the dough is smooth and elastic.
4. Place the dough in a greased bowl, cover it with a clean kitchen towel, and let it rest in a warm place for about 1 hour or until it doubles in size.
5. After the dough has risen, punch it down to release the air, and transfer it back to the floured surface.
6. Shape the dough into a loaf and place it in the air fryer basket lined with parchment paper.
7. Set the air fryer temperature to 180°C and the cooking time to 20-25 minutes.
8. Once cooked, carefully remove the **Potato Bread** from the air fryer and let it cool on a wire rack before slicing.

Cheese Twists

Prep: 15 Min | Cook: 10 Min | Serves: 12 twists

Ingredient:

- 250g puff pastry, thawed if frozen
- 1 tablespoon Dijon mustard
- 100g grated cheddar cheese
- 1 teaspoon paprika
- 1 teaspoon dried thyme
- 1 egg, beaten (for egg wash)

Instruction:

1. Roll out the puff pastry on a lightly floured surface into a rectangle about 30cm x 20cm and approximately 3mm thick.
2. Spread the Dijon mustard evenly over the surface of the puff pastry.
3. Sprinkle the grated cheddar cheese, paprika, and dried thyme evenly over the mustard-covered pastry.
4. Fold the puff pastry in half lengthwise, pressing lightly to seal the edges.
5. Using a sharp knife or a pizza cutter, cut the pastry into strips about 1.5cm wide.
6. Take each strip and twist it gently, then place it on a baking tray lined with parchment paper.
7. Place the cheese twists in the air fryer basket, ensuring they are not touching.
8. Cook the cheese twists in the air fryer at 180°C for about 10 minutes, or until they are puffed up and golden brown.
9. Remove the cheese twists from the air fryer and let them cool slightly on a wire rack.
10. Serve your delicious **Cheese Twists** warm as a delightful snack or as an appetizer for gatherings!

Chapter 05: Breads

Pretzel Bites

Prep: 90 Min | Cook: 12 Min | Serves: 4

Ingredient:

- 300g strong white bread flour
- 1 tsp instant yeast
- 1 tsp sugar
- 1/2 tsp salt
- 1 tbsp olive oil
- 180ml warm water
- 1.5 liters water
- 2 tbsp baking soda
- 2 tbsp unsalted butter, melted
- Coarse sea salt, for sprinkling

Instruction:

1. In a mixing bowl, combine the bread flour, instant yeast, sugar, and salt.
2. Add the olive oil and warm water to the bowl and mix until a soft dough forms. Transfer the dough to a floured surface and knead for about 10 minutes until the dough is smooth and elastic. Let dough rise for 1 hour.
3. After the dough has risen, punch it down to release the air, and transfer it back to the floured surface. Divide the dough into small pieces and roll each piece into a ball, about 2-3 cm in diameter.
4. In a large saucepan, bring the water to a boil. Once boiling, add the baking soda and stir until dissolved.
5. Boil dough balls for 30 seconds and drain.
6. Place the pretzel bites in the air fryer basket, leaving a little space between each bite. You may need to cook them in batches depending on the size of your air fryer.
7. Set the air fryer temperature to 180°C and the cooking time to 10-12 minutes.
8. Once cooked, remove the pretzel bites from the air fryer and brush them with melted butter. Sprinkle with coarse sea salt while they're still warm. Serve the **Pretzel Bites** warm as they are or with your favorite dipping sauce.

Instruction:

1. In a mixing bowl, combine the strong white bread flour, salt, and instant yeast.
2. Gradually add the warm water to the flour mixture, mixing with your hands or a spoon, until a soft and slightly sticky dough forms. Adjust the amount of water or flour as needed.
3. Transfer the dough onto a lightly floured surface and knead it for about 10 minutes until smooth and elastic.
4. Shape the dough into a round loaf by folding the edges towards the center, rotating the dough as you go.
5. Grease the air fryer basket with olive oil and place the shaped loaf inside, seam side down.
6. Cook the bread in the air fryer at 180°C for about 25 minutes, or until it is golden brown and sounds hollow when tapped on the bottom.
7. Remove the bread from the air fryer and let it cool on a wire rack before slicing.
8. Serve your homemade **Artisan Bread** and enjoy it as a tasty addition to your meals or as a base for sandwiches!

Artisan Bread

Prep: 15 Min | Cook: 25 Min | Serves: 1 loaf

Ingredient:

- 500g strong white bread flour
- 10g salt
- 7g instant yeast
- 350ml warm water (adjust as needed)
- Olive oil, for greasing

Chapter 05: Breads

Sourdough Discs

Prep: 15 Min | Cook: 15 Min | Serves: 4

Ingredient:

- 250g strong white bread flour
- 150g active sourdough starter
- 150g lukewarm water
- 5g salt
- Olive oil (for greasing)

Instruction:

1. In a large mixing bowl, combine the bread flour and salt. Make a well in the center.
2. Add the active sourdough starter and lukewarm water into the well. Mix everything together using a wooden spoon or your hands until a shaggy dough forms.
3. Transfer the dough onto a lightly floured surface and knead for about 10 minutes until the dough becomes smooth and elastic.
4. Divide the dough into 4 equal portions and shape each portion into a ball. Flatten each ball into a disc shape, approximately 1.5cm thick.
5. Lightly grease the air fryer basket with olive oil to prevent sticking. Place the sourdough discs in a single layer in the basket, leaving some space between them.
6. Set the air fryer to 180°C and cook the discs for 15 minutes until they turn golden brown and crispy. You may need to cook them in batches depending on the size of your air fryer.
7. Once cooked, remove the sourdough discs from the air fryer and let them cool on a wire rack for a few minutes.
8. Serve the **Sourdough Discs** warm or at room temperature as a delicious accompaniment to soups, salads, or as a base for sandwiches.

Instruction:

1. Slice the baguette into 1.5cm thick slices. Set aside.
2. In a small bowl, combine the olive oil, minced garlic (if using), salt, and black pepper. Mix well.
3. Brush both sides of each baguette slice with the seasoned olive oil mixture. Ensure that each slice is evenly coated.
4. Place the baguette slices in a single layer in the air fryer basket. You may need to cook them in batches depending on the size of your air fryer.
5. Set the air fryer to 180°C and cook the baguette slices for 5 minutes. Flip the slices over and cook for an additional 5 minutes until they turn golden brown and crispy.
6. Once cooked, remove the baguette slices from the air fryer and transfer them to a serving plate.
7. Garnish with fresh herbs, if desired, and serve the baguette slices warm as a delightful accompaniment to soups, dips, or as a base for bruschetta.
8. Enjoy your homemade baguette slices prepared in the air fryer with a **British twist!**

British Twist

Prep: 10 Min | Cook: 10 Min | Serves: 4

Ingredient:

- 1 baguette (about 250g), preferably day-old
- 2 tablespoons olive oil
- 1 clove garlic, minced (optional)
- Salt, to taste
- Freshly ground black pepper, to taste
- Fresh herbs (such as parsley or thyme), for garnish (optional)

Chapter 05: Breads

Cinnamon Swirl Bread

Prep: 20 Min | Cook: 25 Min | Serves: 1 loaf

Ingredient:

- 500g strong white bread flour
- 10g instant yeast
- 50g sugar
- 1 teaspoon salt
- 50g unsalted butter, melted
- 300ml warm milk
- 1 egg, beaten
- 50g softened butter
- 75g brown sugar
- 2 teaspoons ground cinnamon
- 1 tablespoon granulated sugar
- 1/2 teaspoon ground cinnamon

Instruction:

1. In a mixing bowl, combine the strong white bread flour, instant yeast, sugar, and salt.
2. Add the melted butter, warm milk, and beaten egg to the bowl. Mix until a dough forms.
3. Transfer the dough onto a lightly floured surface and knead it for about 10 minutes until smooth and elastic.
4. Place the dough in a greased bowl, cover with a clean kitchen towel, and let it rise in a warm place for about 1 hour or until doubled in size.
5. After the dough has risen, punch it down and roll it out into a rectangle approximately 30cm x 20cm.
6. In a small bowl, mix together the softened butter, brown sugar, and ground cinnamon to make the cinnamon swirl filling.
7. Spread the cinnamon swirl filling evenly over the rolled-out dough. Starting from one of the long sides, tightly roll up the dough into a log shape.
8. Place the rolled dough into the air fryer basket, seam side down. Cook at 180°C for 25 minutes until golden brown.
9. Brush the top with melted butter and sprinkle with the mixture of granulated sugar and ground cinnamon.
10. Let it cool on a wire rack before slicing. Enjoy your homemade **Cinnamon Swirl Bread!**

Instruction:

1. In a mixing bowl, combine the bread flour, wholemeal flour, hemp seeds, instant yeast, sugar, and salt.
2. Add the olive oil and warm water to the bowl, and mix until a soft dough forms.
3. Transfer the dough to a floured surface and knead for about 10 minutes until the dough is smooth and elastic.
4. Place the dough in a greased bowl, cover it with a clean kitchen towel, and let it rest in a warm place for about 1 hour or until it doubles in size.
5. After the dough has risen, punch it down to release the air, and transfer it back to the floured surface.
6. Shape the dough into a loaf and place it in the air fryer basket lined with parchment paper.
7. Set the air fryer temperature to 180°C and the cooking time to 30-35 minutes.
8. Once cooked, carefully remove the **Hemp seed Bread** from the air fryer and let it cool on a wire rack before slicing.

Hemp seed Bread

Prep: 120 Min | Cook: 35 Min | Serves: 1 loaf

Ingredient:

- 300g strong white bread flour
- 100g wholemeal flour
- 50g hemp seeds
- 1 tsp instant yeast
- 1 tsp sugar
- 1 tsp salt
- 1 tbsp olive oil
- 280ml warm water

Chapter 05: Breads

Spelt Flour Buns

Prep: 150 Min | Cook: 15 Min | Serves: 6 bnus

Ingredient:

- 300g spelt flour
- 1 tsp instant yeast
- 1 tsp sugar
- 1/2 tsp salt
- 1 tbsp olive oil
- 180ml warm water
- Sesame seeds or poppy seeds for topping (optional)

Instruction:

1. In a mixing bowl, combine the spelt flour, instant yeast, sugar, and salt.
2. Add the olive oil and warm water to the bowl and mix until a soft dough forms. Transfer the dough to a floured surface and knead for about 10 minutes until the dough is smooth and elastic.
3. Place the dough in a greased bowl, cover it with a clean kitchen towel, and let it rest in a warm place for about 2 hours or until it doubles in size.
4. After the dough has risen, punch it down to release the air, and transfer it back to the floured surface. Divide the dough into 6 equal portions and shape each portion into a bun.
5. Place the buns in the air fryer basket, leaving a little space between each bun. You may need to cook them in batches depending on the size of your air fryer.
6. Set the air fryer temperature to 180°C and the cooking time to 12-15 minutes.
7. Once cooked, remove the **Spelt Flour Buns** from the air fryer and let them cool on a wire rack. Optional: Brush the tops of the buns with a little water and sprinkle sesame seeds or poppy seeds on top for added flavor and texture.

Instruction:

1. In a large mixing bowl, combine the bread flour, instant yeast, sugar, and salt. Mix well.
2. Make a well in the center of the dry ingredients and pour in the lukewarm water and olive oil. Stir until a dough forms.
3. Transfer the dough onto a lightly floured surface and knead for about 5-7 minutes until the dough becomes smooth and elastic.
4. Divide the dough into small portions and shape each portion into a bite-sized ball, approximately 2-3cm in diameter.
5. Place the pizza dough bites in a single layer in the air fryer basket. Leave some space between them as they will expand during cooking.
6. Set the air fryer to 180°C and cook the pizza dough bites for 10 minutes until they turn golden brown and crispy.
7. Once cooked, remove the pizza dough bites from the air fryer and let them cool for a few minutes.
8. Serve the **Pizza Dough Bites** with tomato pizza sauce for dipping. If desired, you can also sprinkle grated cheese and your favorite toppings over the bites before cooking them in the air fryer.

Pizza Dough Bites

Prep: 20 Min | Cook: 10 Min | Serves: 4

Ingredient:

- 250g strong white bread flour
- 1 teaspoon instant yeast
- 1 teaspoon sugar
- 1/2 teaspoon salt
- 150ml lukewarm water
- 2 tablespoons olive oil
- Tomato pizza sauce, for dipping
- Grated cheese, for topping (optional)
- Toppings of your choice (such as chopped vegetables, cooked meat, or herbs)

Chapter 05: Breads

Buttery Soft Rolls

Prep: 15 Min | Cook: 12 Min | Serves: 8 rolls

Ingredient:

- 500g strong white bread flour
- 7g fast-action yeast
- 30g sugar
- 1 teaspoon salt
- 60g unsalted butter, softened
- 300ml lukewarm water
- Extra butter, for brushing

Instruction:

1. In a large mixing bowl, combine the bread flour, fast-action yeast, sugar, and salt. Mix well.
2. Add the softened butter to the dry ingredients and rub it in using your fingertips until the mixture resembles fine breadcrumbs.
3. Make a well in the center of the mixture and gradually add the lukewarm water. Stir until a soft dough forms.
4. Transfer the dough onto a lightly floured surface and knead for about 10 minutes until the dough becomes smooth and elastic.
5. Divide the dough into 8 equal portions and shape each portion into a round roll. Place the rolls on a greased baking tray, leaving some space between them.
6. Place the baking tray with the rolls in the air fryer basket. You may need to cook them in batches depending on the size of your air fryer.
7. Set the air fryer to 180°C and cook the rolls for 12 minutes until they turn golden brown and sound hollow when tapped on the bottom.
8. Once cooked, remove the **Buttery Soft Rolls** from the air fryer and transfer them to a wire rack. Brush the tops of the rolls with melted butter for extra richness and shine.
9. Allow the rolls to cool slightly before serving. They are best enjoyed warm and fresh.

Tomato Basil Flatbread

Prep: 15 Min | Cook: 10 Min | Serves: 4

Ingredient:

- 200g plain flour
- 1 tsp baking powder
- 1/2 tsp salt
- 1/2 tsp dried basil
- 2 tbsp olive oil
- 100ml warm water
- 4-5 cherry tomatoes, sliced
- Fresh basil leaves, torn
- Salt and pepper, to taste

Instruction:

1. In a mixing bowl, combine the plain flour, baking powder, salt, and dried basil.
2. Add the olive oil and warm water to the bowl and mix until a soft dough forms.
3. Transfer the dough to a floured surface and knead for about 5 minutes until the dough is smooth and elastic.
4. Divide the dough into 2 or 4 equal portions, depending on the desired size of your flatbreads.
5. Roll each portion of dough into a thin circle or oval shape, approximately 0.5 cm thick.
6. Place the flatbreads in the air fryer basket, leaving a little space between each one. You may need to cook them in batches depending on the size of your air fryer.
7. Arrange the sliced cherry tomatoes on top of the flatbreads, and sprinkle with torn basil leaves, salt, and pepper.
8. Set the air fryer temperature to 180°C and the cooking time to 8-10 minutes.
9. Once cooked, remove the **Tomato Basil Flatbread** from the air fryer and let them cool slightly before serving.

Chapter 05: Breads

Cheese and Herb Focaccia

Prep: 20 Min | Cook: 12 Min | Serves: 8 slices

Ingredient:

- 400g strong white bread flour
- 7g fast-action yeast
- 1 teaspoon sugar
- 1 teaspoon salt
- 250ml lukewarm water
- 3 tablespoons olive oil
- 100g grated cheese (such as Cheddar or mozzarella)
- 2 tablespoons fresh herbs (such as rosemary or thyme), chopped
- Coarse sea salt, for sprinkling

Instruction:

1. In a large mixing bowl, combine the bread flour, fast-action yeast, sugar, and salt. Mix well.
2. Add the lukewarm water and 2 tablespoons of olive oil to the dry ingredients. Stir until a soft dough forms.
3. Transfer the dough onto a lightly floured surface and knead for about 10 minutes until the dough becomes smooth and elastic.
4. Place the dough in a greased bowl, cover with a clean kitchen towel, and let it rise in a warm place for about 1 hour or until doubled in size.
5. Once the dough has risen, punch it down to release the air. Transfer it to a greased air fryer basket or tray. Gently press and stretch the dough to fit the basket or tray evenly.
6. Drizzle the remaining 1 tablespoon of olive oil over the dough. Sprinkle the grated cheese, chopped herbs, and coarse sea salt evenly on top.
7. Set the air fryer to 180°C and cook the focaccia for 12 minutes until it turns golden brown and the cheese is melted and bubbly.
8. Once cooked, remove the focaccia from the air fryer and let it cool slightly before slicing into wedges or squares.
9. Serve the **Cheese and Herb Focaccia** warm as a delightful appetizer or accompaniment to soups, salads, or pasta dishes.

Instruction:

1. In a mixing bowl, combine the plain flour, baking powder, salt, 1 tbsp granulated sugar, and 1 tsp ground cinnamon.
2. Add the melted butter and warm water to the bowl and mix until a soft dough forms. Transfer the dough to a floured surface and knead for about 5 minutes until the dough is smooth and elastic. Roll the dough into a thin rectangle shape, approximately 0.5 cm thick.
3. In a separate bowl, combine the 2 tbsp granulated sugar and 1 tsp ground cinnamon for coating. Brush the surface of the dough with a little water, then sprinkle the cinnamon sugar mixture evenly over the dough.
4. Gently press the cinnamon sugar mixture into the dough to ensure it adheres.
5. Cut the dough into smaller rectangular or triangular pieces, as desired. Place the cinnamon sugar flatbread pieces in the air fryer basket, leaving a little space between each one. You may need to cook them in batches depending on the size of your air fryer.
6. Set the air fryer temperature to 180°C and the cooking time to 8-10 minutes.
7. Once cooked, remove the **Cinnamon Sugar Flatbread** from the air fryer and let them cool slightly before serving.

Cinnamon Sugar Flatbread

Prep: 10 Min | Cook: 10 Min | Serves: 4

Ingredient:

- 200g plain flour
- 1 tsp baking powder
- 1/4 tsp salt
- 1 tbsp granulated sugar
- 1 tsp ground cinnamon
- 2 tbsp melted butter
- 100ml warm water
- 2 tbsp granulated sugar (for coating)
- 1 tsp ground cinnamon (for coating)

Chapter 05: Breads

Fruit and Nut Bread Slices

Prep: 15 Min | Cook: 15 Min | Serves: 6 slices

Ingredient:

- 250g strong white bread flour
- 7g fast-action yeast
- 25g sugar
- 1/2 teaspoon salt
- 150ml lukewarm water
- 2 tablespoons olive oil
- 75g dried fruit (such as raisins or cranberries)
- 50g chopped nuts (such as walnuts or almonds)
- 1 tablespoon honey, for glazing (optional)

Instruction:

1. In a large mixing bowl, combine the bread flour, fast-action yeast, sugar, and salt. Mix well.
2. Add the lukewarm water and olive oil to the dry ingredients. Stir until a soft dough forms.
3. Transfer the dough onto a lightly floured surface and knead for about 10 minutes until the dough becomes smooth and elastic.
4. Flatten the dough into a rectangle shape and sprinkle the dried fruit and chopped nuts evenly over the surface.
5. Roll up the dough tightly, sealing the edges as you go. Place the rolled dough in a greased air fryer basket or tray.
6. Set the air fryer to 180°C and cook the bread for 15 minutes until it turns golden brown and sounds hollow when tapped on the bottom.
7. Once cooked, remove the bread from the air fryer and let it cool slightly. If desired, brush the top of the bread with honey for a shiny glaze.
8. Slice the fruit and nut bread into 6 thick slices.
9. Serve the **Fruit and Nut Bread Slices** as a delicious breakfast or snack. They can be enjoyed plain or with a spread of butter or jam.

Instruction:

1. In a mixing bowl, combine the bread flour, instant yeast, sugar, and salt.
2. Add the olive oil and warm water to the bowl and mix until a soft dough forms. Transfer the dough to a floured surface and knead for about 10 minutes until the dough is smooth and elastic.
3. Place the dough in a greased bowl, cover it with a clean kitchen towel, and let it rest in a warm place for about 2 hours or until it doubles in size.
4. After the dough has risen, punch it down to release the air, and transfer it back to the floured surface. Roll the dough into a rectangle or oval shape, approximately 1 cm thick.
5. Place the dough in the air fryer basket, leaving a little space around the edges for expansion.
6. Press the halved black olives into the dough, sprinkle fresh rosemary leaves on top, and lightly press them into the dough as well.
7. Set the air fryer temperature to 180°C and the cooking time to 12-15 minutes.
8. Once cooked, remove the **Olive and Rosemary Focaccia** from the air fryer and sprinkle with coarse sea salt. Let the focaccia cool slightly before slicing and serving.

Olive and Rosemary Focaccia

Prep: 150 Min | Cook: 15 Min | Serves: 4

Ingredient:

- 300g strong white bread flour
- 1 tsp instant yeast
- 1 tsp sugar
- 1 tsp salt
- 1 tbsp olive oil
- 200ml warm water
- 50g pitted black olives, halved
- Fresh rosemary leaves
- Coarse sea salt, for sprinkling

Chapter 05: Breads

Mint Julep Donuts

Prep: 20 Min | Cook: 10 Min | Serves: 12 donuts

Ingredient:

- 250g plain flour
- 50g caster sugar
- 2 teaspoons baking powder
- 1/4 teaspoon salt
- 120ml milk
- 1 large egg
- 2 tablespoons unsalted butter, melted
- Vegetable oil, for air frying
- 200g icing sugar
- 2 tablespoons fresh mint leaves, finely chopped
- 2 tablespoons bourbon (optional)
- 1-2 tablespoons milk

Instruction:

1. In a mixing bowl, whisk together the plain flour, caster sugar, baking powder, and salt. In a separate bowl, whisk together the milk, egg, and melted butter. Pour the wet ingredients into the dry ingredients and stir until just combined. Do not overmix.
2. Lightly flour a clean surface and roll out the dough to a thickness of about 1.5cm. Use a donut cutter or a round cookie cutter to cut out donut shapes. If you don't have a donut cutter, you can use a round cutter for the outer shape and a smaller cutter to make the center hole.
3. Place the donuts on a baking sheet lined with parchment paper.
4. Lightly brush the donuts with vegetable oil on both sides. Place the donuts in a single layer in the air fryer basket. You may need to cook them in batches depending on the size of your air fryer. Cook the donuts in the air fryer to 180°C for 8-10 minutes, flipping them halfway through, until they are golden brown and cooked through.
5. While the donuts are cooling, prepare the mint julep glaze. In a bowl, whisk together the icing sugar, finely chopped fresh mint leaves, bourbon (if using), and enough milk to achieve a thick yet pourable consistency.
6. Dip the cooled donuts into the glaze, allowing any excess glaze to drip off. Place the glazed **Donuts** on a wire rack to set for a few minutes.

Lemon Zest Donuts

Prep: 15 Min | Cook: 8 Min | Serves: 6 donuts

Ingredient:

- 200g plain flour
- 60g caster sugar
- 1 teaspoon baking powder
- 1/4 teaspoon salt
- Zest of 1 lemon
- 120ml milk
- 1 large egg
- 2 tablespoons unsalted butter, melted
- 1/2 teaspoon vanilla extract
- Icing sugar, for dusting

Instruction:

1. In a mixing bowl, combine the plain flour, caster sugar, baking powder, salt, and lemon zest. Mix well.
2. In a separate bowl, whisk together the milk, egg, melted butter, and vanilla extract.
3. Pour the wet ingredients into the dry ingredients. Stir until just combined, being careful not to overmix.
4. Spoon the batter into a greased donut mold, filling each cavity about three-quarters full.
5. Place the donut mold in the air fryer basket. You may need to cook them in batches depending on the size of your air fryer.
6. Set the air fryer to 180°C and cook the donuts for 8 minutes until they turn golden brown and spring back when lightly pressed.
7. Once cooked, remove the donuts from the air fryer and let them cool slightly.
8. Dust the donuts with icing sugar for a sweet finishing touch.
9. Serve the lemon zest donuts as a delightful treat with a cup of tea or coffee.
10. Enjoy your homemade **Lemon Zest Donuts** prepared in the air fryer with a British touch!

Rum Raisin Donuts

Prep: 20 Min | Cook: 8 Min | Serves: 6 donuts

Ingredient:

- 200g plain flour
- 60g caster sugar
- 1 teaspoon baking powder
- 1/4 teaspoon salt
- 1/4 teaspoon ground nutmeg
- 1/4 teaspoon ground cinnamon
- 50g raisins
- 2 tablespoons rum
- 120ml milk
- 1 large egg
- 2 tablespoons unsalted butter, melted
- 1/2 teaspoon vanilla extract
- Icing sugar, for dusting

Instruction:

1. In a small bowl, combine the raisins and rum. Let them soak for about 10 minutes until the raisins plump up. In a mixing bowl, combine the plain flour, caster sugar, baking powder, salt, ground nutmeg, and ground cinnamon. Mix well.
2. In a separate bowl, whisk together the milk, egg, melted butter, and vanilla extract.
3. Drain the raisins from the rum and add them to the wet ingredients. Stir to combine. Pour the wet ingredients into the dry ingredients. Stir until just combined, being careful not to overmix.
4. Spoon the batter into a greased donut mold, filling each cavity about three-quarters full.
5. Place the donut mold in the air fryer basket. You may need to cook them in batches depending on the size of your air fryer.
6. Set the air fryer to 180°C and cook the donuts for 8 minutes until they turn golden brown and spring back when lightly pressed.
7. Once cooked, remove the donuts from the air fryer and let them cool slightly.
8. Dust the donuts with icing sugar for a sweet finishing touch.
9. Serve the **Rum Raisin Donuts** as a delicious treat with a cup of tea or coffee.

Instruction:

1. In a mixing bowl, whisk together the plain flour, baking powder, baking soda, salt, ground ginger, ground cinnamon, ground nutmeg, and ground cloves.
2. In a separate bowl, mix together the melted butter, light brown sugar, egg, milk, and black treacle/molasses until well combined.
3. Add the wet ingredients to the dry ingredients and stir until just combined. Do not overmix.
4. Spoon the batter into a piping bag or a sealable plastic bag with the tip cut off to create a makeshift piping bag.
5. Pipe the batter into the cavities of a greased donut pan, filling each one about 2/3 full.
6. Place the donut pan in the air fryer basket, leaving a little space around each donut. You may need to cook them in batches depending on the size of your air fryer.
7. Set the air fryer temperature to 180°C and the cooking time to 8-10 minutes.
8. Once cooked, remove the gingerbread donuts from the air fryer and let them cool slightly before removing them from the donut pan.
9. Repeat steps 5-8 for any remaining batter.
10. Optional: Dust the **Gingerbread Donuts** with icing sugar for added sweetness and decoration.

Gingerbread Donuts

Prep: 15 Min | Cook: 10 Min | Serves: 6 donuts

Ingredient:

- 200g plain flour
- 1 tsp baking powder
- 1/4 tsp baking soda
- 1/4 tsp salt
- 1 tsp ground ginger
- 1/2 tsp ground cinnamon
- 1/4 tsp ground nutmeg
- 1/4 tsp ground cloves
- 50g unsalted butter, melted
- 80g light brown sugar
- 1 large egg
- 120ml milk
- 2 tbsp black treacle or molasses
- Icing sugar, for dusting (optional)

Chapter 06: Donuts

Coconut Lime Donuts

Prep: 20 Min | Cook: 8 Min | Serves: 6 donuts

Ingredient:

- 200g plain flour
- 60g caster sugar
- 1 teaspoon baking powder
- 1/4 teaspoon salt
- Zest of 1 lime
- 50g desiccated coconut
- 120ml milk
- 1 large egg
- 2 tablespoons unsalted butter, melted
- 1/2 teaspoon vanilla extract
- Icing sugar, for dusting
- Lime zest, for garnish (optional)

Instruction:

1. In a mixing bowl, combine the plain flour, caster sugar, baking powder, salt, lime zest, and desiccated coconut. Mix well.
2. In a separate bowl, whisk together the milk, egg, melted butter, and vanilla extract.
3. Pour the wet ingredients into the dry ingredients. Stir until just combined, being careful not to overmix.
4. Spoon the batter into a greased donut mold, filling each cavity about three-quarters full.
5. Place the donut mold in the air fryer basket. You may need to cook them in batches depending on the size of your air fryer.
6. Set the air fryer to 180°C and cook the donuts for 8 minutes until they turn golden brown and spring back when lightly pressed.
7. Once cooked, remove the donuts from the air fryer and let them cool slightly.
8. Dust the donuts with icing sugar for a sweet finishing touch. You can also sprinkle some additional lime zest on top for extra flavor and decoration.
9. Serve the coconut lime donuts as a delightful tropical treat with a cup of tea or coffee.
10. Enjoy your homemade **Coconut Lime Donuts** prepared in the air fryer with a British touch!

Instruction:

1. In a mixing bowl, whisk together the plain flour, baking powder, baking soda, and salt.
2. In a separate bowl, mix together the melted butter, granulated sugar, egg, milk, and almond extract until well combined.
3. Add the wet ingredients to the dry ingredients and stir until just combined. Do not overmix.
4. Fold in the chopped glace cherries and flaked almonds into the batter.
5. Spoon the batter into a piping bag or a sealable plastic bag with the tip cut off to create a makeshift piping bag.
6. Pipe the batter into the cavities of a greased donut pan, filling each one about 2/3 full.
7. Place the donut pan in the air fryer basket, leaving a little space around each donut. You may need to cook them in batches depending on the size of your air fryer.
8. Set the air fryer temperature to 180°C and the cooking time to 8-10 minutes.
9. Once cooked, remove the **Cherry Almond Donuts** from the air fryer and let them cool slightly before removing them from the donut pan.
10. Repeat steps 5-9 for any remaining batter.

Cherry Almond Donuts

Prep: 15 Min | Cook: 10 Min | Serves: 6 donuts

Ingredient:

- 200g plain flour
- 1 tsp baking powder
- 1/4 tsp baking soda
- 1/4 tsp salt
- 50g unsalted butter, melted
- 80g granulated sugar
- 1 large egg
- 120ml milk
- 1 tsp almond extract
- 50g glace cherries, chopped
- 25g flaked almonds

Chapter 06: Donuts

Caramel Pecan Donuts

Prep: 20 Min | Cook: 8 Min | Serves: 6 donuts

Ingredient:

- 200g plain flour
- 60g caster sugar
- 1 teaspoon baking powder
- 1/4 teaspoon salt
- 60ml milk
- 1 large egg
- 2 tablespoons unsalted butter, melted
- 1/2 teaspoon vanilla extract
- 50g chopped pecans
- 6 teaspoons caramel sauce
- Icing sugar, for dusting

Instruction:

1. In a mixing bowl, combine the plain flour, caster sugar, baking powder, and salt. Mix well.
2. In a separate bowl, whisk together the milk, egg, melted butter, and vanilla extract.
3. Pour the wet ingredients into the dry ingredients. Stir until just combined, being careful not to overmix.
4. Fold in the chopped pecans into the batter.
5. Spoon half of the batter into a greased donut mold, filling each cavity about halfway. Add a teaspoon of caramel sauce to each cavity, then spoon the remaining batter on top, filling each cavity about three-quarters full.
6. Place the donut mold in the air fryer basket. You may need to cook them in batches depending on the size of your air fryer.
7. Set the air fryer to 180°C and cook the donuts for 8 minutes until they turn golden brown and spring back when lightly pressed.
8. Once cooked, remove the donuts from the air fryer and let them cool slightly.
9. Dust the donuts with icing sugar for a sweet finishing touch.
10. Serve the **Caramel Pecan Donuts** as a delightful treat with a cup of tea or coffee.

Mango Coconut Donuts

Prep: 15 Min | Cook: 10 Min | Serves: 6 donuts

Ingredient:

- 200g plain flour
- 1 tsp baking powder
- 1/4 tsp baking soda
- 1/4 tsp salt
- 50g unsalted butter, melted
- 80g granulated sugar
- 1 large egg
- 120ml coconut milk
- 1 tsp vanilla extract
- 100g ripe mango, finely diced
- 25g desiccated coconut

Instruction:

1. In a mixing bowl, whisk together the plain flour, baking powder, baking soda, and salt.
2. In a separate bowl, mix together the melted butter, granulated sugar, egg, coconut milk, and vanilla extract until well combined.
3. Add the wet ingredients to the dry ingredients and stir until just combined. Do not overmix.
4. Fold in the diced mango and desiccated coconut into the batter.
5. Spoon the batter into a piping bag or a sealable plastic bag with the tip cut off to create a makeshift piping bag.
6. Pipe the batter into the cavities of a greased donut pan, filling each one about 2/3 full.
7. Place the donut pan in the air fryer basket, leaving a little space around each donut. You may need to cook them in batches depending on the size of your air fryer.
8. Set the air fryer temperature to 180°C and the cooking time to 8-10 minutes.
9. Once cooked, remove the **Mango Coconut Donuts** from the air fryer and let them cool slightly before removing them from the donut pan.
10. Repeat steps 5-9 for any remaining batter.

Chapter 06: Donuts

Pecan Praline Donuts

Prep: 20 Min | Cook: 8 Min | Serves: 6 donuts

Ingredient:

- 200g plain flour
- 60g caster sugar
- 1 tsp baking powder
- 1/4 tsp salt
- 60ml milk
- 1 large egg
- 2 tbsp melted unsalted butter
- 1/2 tsp vanilla extract
- 50g chopped pecans
- 60g brown sugar
- 30g unsalted butter
- 2 tbsp double cream
- Icing sugar, for dusting

Instruction:

1. In a mixing bowl, combine flour, caster sugar, baking powder, and salt. Mix well.
2. In a separate bowl, whisk together milk, egg, melted butter, and vanilla extract.
3. Pour wet ingredients into dry ingredients. Stir until just combined.
4. Fold in chopped pecans.
5. Spoon batter into greased donut mold, filling each cavity three-quarters full.
6. Place the mold in the air fryer basket.
7. Set the air fryer to 180°C and cook for 8 minutes until golden brown.
8. While donuts cook, prepare pecan praline topping: melt butter in a saucepan, add brown sugar and double cream, stir until thickened.
9. Remove cooked donuts from the air fryer and let them cool slightly.
10. Drizzle the pecan praline topping over the donuts, allowing it to drip down the sides.
11. Dust the donuts with icing sugar for a sweet finishing touch.
12. Serve the **Pecan Praline Donuts** as a delectable treat with a cup of tea or coffee.

Bourbon Pecan Pie Donuts

Prep: 25 Min | Cook: 8 Min | Serves: 6 donuts

Ingredient:

- 200g plain flour
- 60g caster sugar
- 1 teaspoon baking powder
- 1/4 teaspoon salt
- 60ml milk
- 1 large egg
- 2 tablespoons unsalted butter, melted
- 1/2 teaspoon vanilla extract
- 50g chopped pecans
- 50g unsalted butter
- 50g light brown sugar
- 2 tablespoons double cream
- 1 tablespoon bourbon (optional)
- 50g chopped pecans

Instruction:

1. In a mixing bowl, combine the plain flour, caster sugar, baking powder, and salt. Mix well.
2. In a separate bowl, whisk together the milk, egg, melted butter, and vanilla extract.
3. Pour the wet ingredients into the dry ingredients. Stir until just combined, being careful not to overmix.
4. Fold in the chopped pecans into the batter.
5. Spoon the batter into a greased donut mold, filling each cavity about three-quarters full.
6. Place the donut mold in the air fryer basket. You may need to cook them in batches depending on the size of your air fryer.
7. Set the air fryer to 180°C and cook the donuts for 8 minutes until they turn golden brown and spring back when lightly pressed.
8. While the donuts are cooking, prepare the bourbon pecan pie topping. In a saucepan, melt the unsalted butter over medium heat. Add the light brown sugar and double cream, stirring until the sugar has dissolved and the mixture has thickened slightly. Remove **Bourbon Pecan Pie Donuts** from the air fryer and let them cool slightly.
9. Drizzle bourbon pecan pie topping over the donuts.

Chapter 06: Donuts

Chocolate Mint Donuts

Prep: 15 Min | Cook: 10 Min | Serves: 12 donuts

Ingredient:

- 200g self-raising flour
- 100g caster sugar
- 2 tbsp cocoa powder
- 150ml whole milk
- 2 large eggs
- 75g unsalted butter, melted
- 1 tsp vanilla extract
- A pinch of salt
- 1/2 tsp peppermint extract
- Green food coloring (optional)
- 150g icing sugar
- Chocolate shavings or sprinkles (optional)
- 1-2 tbsp milk

Instruction:

1. In a large mixing bowl, whisk together the self-raising flour, caster sugar, cocoa powder, and a pinch of salt.
2. In a separate bowl, combine the melted butter, whole milk, eggs, and vanilla extract. Mix until well combined.
3. Pour the wet ingredients into the dry ingredients and gently fold until just combined. Do not overmix. Spoon the batter into a donut pan, filling each cavity about two-thirds full.
4. Place the donut pan in the air fryer basket. Be sure to leave some space between each donut for even cooking.
5. Cook the donuts in the air fryer at 180°C for 8-10 minutes or until a toothpick inserted into the center comes out clean.
6. While the donuts are cooking, prepare the chocolate mint glaze. In a bowl, whisk together the icing sugar, cocoa powder, milk, peppermint extract, and green food coloring (if using) until smooth.
7. Once the donuts are done, allow them to cool in the pan for a few minutes, then transfer them to a wire rack.
8. Dip each donut into the chocolate mint glaze, ensuring they are well-coated. Allow any excess glaze to drip off.
9. If desired, sprinkle chocolate shavings or sprinkles over the glazed donuts. Allow the glaze to set, and then the **Chocolate Mint Donuts** are ready to be enjoyed!

Banana Caramel Donuts

Prep: 15 Min | Cook: 10 Min | Serves: 12 donuts

Ingredient:

- 200g self-raising flour
- 100g caster sugar
- 2 ripe bananas, mashed
- 150ml whole milk
- 2 large eggs
- 75g unsalted butter, melted
- 1 tsp vanilla extract
- A pinch of salt
- 150g icing sugar
- 2 tbsp caramel sauce
- 1-2 tbsp milk
- Chopped nuts or banana slices (optional)

Instruction:

1. In a large mixing bowl, whisk together the self-raising flour, caster sugar, and a pinch of salt.
2. In a separate bowl, combine the mashed bananas, melted butter, whole milk, eggs, and vanilla extract. Mix until well combined. Pour the wet ingredients into the dry ingredients and gently fold until just combined. Do not overmix.
3. Spoon the batter into a donut pan, filling each cavity about two-thirds full.
4. Place the donut pan in the air fryer basket. Be sure to leave some space between each donut for even cooking.
5. Cook the donuts in the air fryer at 180°C for 8-10 minutes or until a toothpick inserted into the center comes out clean.
6. While the donuts are cooking, prepare the caramel glaze. In a bowl, whisk together the icing sugar, caramel sauce, and milk until smooth.
7. Once the donuts are done, allow them to cool in the pan for a few minutes, then transfer them to a wire rack.
8. Dip each donut into the caramel glaze, ensuring they are well-coated. Allow any excess glaze to drip off.
9. If desired, decorate with chopped nuts or banana slices.
10. Allow the glaze to set, and then the **Banana Caramel Donuts** are ready to be enjoyed!

Chapter 06: Donuts

Blueberry Almond Donuts

Prep: 15 Min | Cook: 10 Min | Serves: 12 donuts

Ingredient:

- 250g all-purpose flour
- 1 sachet (7g) instant yeast
- 50g unsalted butter, melted
- 1 large egg
- 150ml whole milk
- 75g granulated sugar
- 1/2 teaspoon almond extract
- 100g fresh blueberries
- A pinch of salt
- Icing sugar for dusting (optional)

Instruction:

1. In a small bowl, whisk together the melted butter, egg, milk, and almond extract.
2. In a large mixing bowl, combine the flour, sugar, yeast, and a pinch of salt.
3. Make a well in the center of the dry ingredients and pour in the wet mixture. Stir until just combined.
4. Gently fold in the fresh blueberries, being careful not to overmix.
5. Spoon the batter into a piping bag or a plastic sandwich bag with a corner snipped off.
6. Lightly grease the air fryer basket with oil.
7. Pipe the batter into the air fryer basket, forming ring shapes to make the donuts.
8. Air fry at 180°C for 8-10 minutes or until the donuts are golden brown and cooked through.
9. Remove the donuts from the air fryer and let them cool on a wire rack.
10. Optional: Dust the cooled donuts with icing sugar for a finishing touch. Serve and enjoy these delightful **Blueberry Almond Donuts**!

Blackberry Jelly Donuts

Prep: 15 Min | Cook: 10 Min | Serves: 12 donuts

Ingredient:

- 300g strong white bread flour
- 50g caster sugar
- 7g fast-action yeast
- 150ml whole milk, lukewarm
- 50g unsalted butter, melted
- 1 large egg
- A pinch of salt
- Blackberry jam or jelly
- Icing sugar

Instruction:

1. In a large mixing bowl, combine the bread flour, caster sugar, and a pinch of salt.
2. In a separate bowl, mix the fast-action yeast with lukewarm whole milk and let it sit for a few minutes until frothy.
3. Add the yeast mixture, melted butter, and beaten egg to the dry ingredients. Mix until a dough forms.
4. Knead the dough on a floured surface for about 10 minutes until it becomes smooth and elastic.
5. Place the dough in a lightly oiled bowl, cover with a damp cloth, and let it rise in a warm place for about 1 hour or until doubled in size. Punch down the risen dough and roll it out on a floured surface to about 1cm thickness.
6. Using a round cutter, cut out circles from the dough. Place a small amount of blackberry jam or jelly in the center of half the circles.
7. Place the remaining circles on top of the jam-filled ones and pinch the edges to seal, creating a filled donut. Place the filled donuts in the air fryer basket, leaving space between each.
8. Cook the donuts in the air fryer at 180°C for 5-7 minutes or until golden brown.
9. Once cooked, remove the donuts from the air fryer, dust with icing sugar, and serve warm. Enoy the **Blackberry Jelly Donuts**.

Cranberry Walnut Donuts

Prep: 15 Min | Cook: 10 Min | Serves: 12 donuts

Ingredient:

- 200g all-purpose flour
- 100g granulated sugar
- 1 tsp baking powder
- 1/2 tsp baking soda
- 1/4 tsp salt
- 120ml buttermilk
- 1 large egg
- 30g unsalted butter, melted
- 1 tsp vanilla extract
- 100g dried cranberries
- 50g chopped walnuts
- 100g icing sugar
- 2-3 tbsp milk

Instruction:

1. In a large bowl, whisk together the flour, sugar, baking powder, baking soda, and salt.
2. In a separate bowl, combine the buttermilk, egg, melted butter, and vanilla extract.
3. Pour the wet ingredients into the dry ingredients, stirring until just combined.
4. Fold in the dried cranberries and chopped walnuts.
5. Spoon the batter into a greased donut pan, filling each mold about 2/3 full.
6. Place the donut pan in the air fryer basket. Set the air fryer to 180°C and cook for 8-10 minutes, or until a toothpick inserted into the donuts comes out clean.
7. While the donuts are cooking, prepare the glaze. In a bowl, whisk together the icing sugar, milk, and vanilla extract until smooth.
8. Once the donuts are done, let them cool in the pan for a few minutes before transferring them to a wire rack.
9. Dip each donut into the glaze, ensuring they are fully coated.
10. Allow the glaze to set for a few minutes before serving **Cranberry Walnut Donuts**.

Chocolate Coconut Donuts

Prep: 20 Min | Cook: 10 Min | Serves: 12 donuts

Instruction:

1. In a large bowl, sift together the flour, cocoa powder, sugar, baking powder, baking soda, and salt.
2. In another bowl, whisk together the buttermilk, eggs, melted butter, and vanilla extract. Add the wet ingredients to the dry ingredients, stirring until just combined.
3. Fold in the shredded coconut.
4. Spoon the batter into a greased donut pan, filling each mold about 2/3 full.
5. Place the donut pan in the air fryer basket. Set the air fryer to 180°C and cook for 8-10 minutes, or until a toothpick inserted into the donuts comes out clean.
6. While the donuts are cooking, prepare the chocolate glaze. In a heatproof bowl over simmering water, melt the dark chocolate, butter, and golden syrup, stirring until smooth.
7. Once the donuts are done, let them cool in the pan for a few minutes before transferring them to a wire rack.
8. Dip each donut into the chocolate glaze, allowing any excess to drip off.
9. Sprinkle additional shredded coconut on top of the glazed donuts.
10. Allow the glaze to set for a few minutes before serving **Chocolate Coconut Donuts**.

Ingredient:

- 200g all-purpose flour
- 50g cocoa powder
- 150g granulated sugar
- 1 tsp baking powder
- 1/2 tsp baking soda
- 1/4 tsp salt
- 180ml buttermilk
- 2 large eggs
- 60g unsalted butter, melted
- 1 tsp vanilla extract
- 50g shredded coconut
- 100g dark chocolate, chopped
- 2 tbsp golden syrup

Coconut Rum Glazed Donuts

Prep: 20 Min | Cook: 10 Min | Serves: 6 donuts

Ingredient:

- 150g all-purpose flour
- 60g granulated sugar
- 1 tsp baking powder
- 1/4 tsp salt
- 60ml coconut milk
- 30ml vegetable oil
- 1 tsp vanilla extract
- 1 large egg
- 100g icing sugar (powdered sugar)
- 2 tbsp coconut rum
- 2-3 tbsp desiccated coconut

Instruction:

1. In a mixing bowl, whisk together the flour, sugar, baking powder, and salt. In a separate bowl, whisk together the coconut milk, vegetable oil, vanilla extract, and egg. Pour the wet ingredients into the dry ingredients and stir until just combined.
2. Spoon the batter into a piping bag or a Ziploc bag with a corner snipped off. Pipe the batter into the donut molds of your air fryer, filling each one about 2/3 full. Air fry at 180°C for about 10 minutes, until golden brown.
3. While the donuts are cooking, prepare the glaze. In a small bowl, whisk together the icing sugar and coconut rum until smooth and well combined.
4. Once the donuts are cooked, remove them from the air fryer and let them cool for a few minutes. Dip the top of each donut into the glaze, allowing any excess to drip off.
5. Sprinkle desiccated coconut over the glazed donuts while the glaze is still wet, allowing it to stick.
6. Place the glazed **Donuts** on a wire rack to allow the glaze to set completely.

Instruction:

1. In a large bowl, whisk together the flour, light brown sugar, baking powder, baking soda, and salt.
2. In another bowl, whisk together the buttermilk, eggs, melted butter, and vanilla extract.
3. Add the wet ingredients to the dry ingredients, stirring until just combined.
4. Fold in the toffee bits and chopped pecans.
5. Spoon the batter into a greased donut pan, filling each mold about 2/3 full.
6. Place the donut pan in the air fryer basket. Set the air fryer to 180°C and cook for 8-10 minutes, or until a toothpick inserted into the donuts comes out clean.
7. While the donuts are cooking, prepare the toffee glaze. In a bowl, whisk together the icing sugar and milk until smooth.
8. Once the donuts are done, let them cool in the pan for a few minutes before transferring them to a wire rack.
9. Dip each donut into the toffee glaze, ensuring they are fully coated.
10. Sprinkle additional toffee bits on top of the glazed donuts for decoration.
11. Allow the glaze to set for a few minutes before serving **Toffee Pecan Donuts**.

Toffee Pecan Donuts

Prep: 15 Min | Cook: 10 Min | Serves: 12 donuts

Ingredient:

- 200g all-purpose flour
- 100g light brown sugar
- 2 tsp baking powder
- 1/2 tsp baking soda
- 1/4 tsp salt
- 150ml buttermilk
- 2 large eggs
- 60g unsalted butter, melted
- 1 tsp vanilla extract
- 100g toffee bits
- 50g chopped pecans
- 150g icing sugar

Chapter 06: Donuts

Passion Fruit Glazed Donuts

Prep: 15 Min | Cook: 10 Min | Serves: 12 donuts

Ingredient:

- 200g all-purpose flour
- 100g granulated sugar
- 2 tsp baking powder
- 1/2 tsp baking soda
- 1/4 tsp salt
- 150ml buttermilk
- 2 large eggs
- 60g unsalted butter, melted
- 1 tsp vanilla extract
- 3-4 passion fruits, pulp extracted
- 200g icing sugar
- 3-4 tbsp passion fruit pulp (from the extracted passion fruits)

Instruction:

1. In a large bowl, whisk together the flour, sugar, baking powder, baking soda, and salt.
2. In another bowl, whisk together the buttermilk, eggs, melted butter, and vanilla extract.
3. Add the wet ingredients to the dry ingredients, stirring until just combined.
4. Spoon the batter into a greased donut pan, filling each mold about 2/3 full.
5. Place the donut pan in the air fryer basket. Set the air fryer to 180°C and cook for 8-10 minutes, or until a toothpick inserted into the donuts comes out clean.
6. While the donuts are cooking, prepare the passion fruit glaze. In a bowl, whisk together the icing sugar and passion fruit pulp until smooth.
7. Once the donuts are done, let them cool in the pan for a few minutes before transferring them to a wire rack.
8. Dip each donut into the passion fruit glaze, ensuring they are fully coated.
9. Allow the glaze to set for a few minutes before serving.
10. Drizzle additional passion fruit pulp on top of the glazed **Donuts** for extra flavor.

Pumpkin Spice Latte Donuts

Prep: 15 Min | Cook: 10 Min | Serves: 12 donuts

Ingredient:

- 200g all-purpose flour
- 100g granulated sugar
- 2 tsp baking powder
- 1/2 tsp baking soda
- 1/4 tsp salt
- 150ml pumpkin puree
- 120ml buttermilk
- 2 tbsp instant coffee granules, dissolved in 1 tbsp hot water
- 1 large egg
- 60g unsalted butter, melted
- 1 tsp vanilla extract
- 1 tsp pumpkin spice mix

Instruction:

1. In a large bowl, whisk together the flour, sugar, baking powder, baking soda, salt, and pumpkin spice mix.
2. In another bowl, combine the pumpkin puree, buttermilk, dissolved coffee, egg, melted butter, and vanilla extract.
3. Add the wet ingredients to the dry ingredients, stirring until just combined.
4. Spoon the batter into a greased donut pan, filling each mold about 2/3 full.
5. Place the donut pan in the air fryer basket. Set the air fryer to 180°C and cook for 8-10 minutes, or until a toothpick inserted into the donuts comes out clean.
6. While the donuts are cooking, prepare the glaze. Whisk together the icing sugar and brewed coffee until smooth.
7. Once the donuts are done, let them cool in the pan for a few minutes before transferring them to a wire rack.
8. Dip each donut into the coffee glaze, ensuring they are fully coated.
9. Allow the glaze to set for a few minutes before serving **Pumpkin Spice Latte Donuts**.
10. Optionally, sprinkle a pinch of pumpkin spice mix on top of the glazed donuts for decoration.

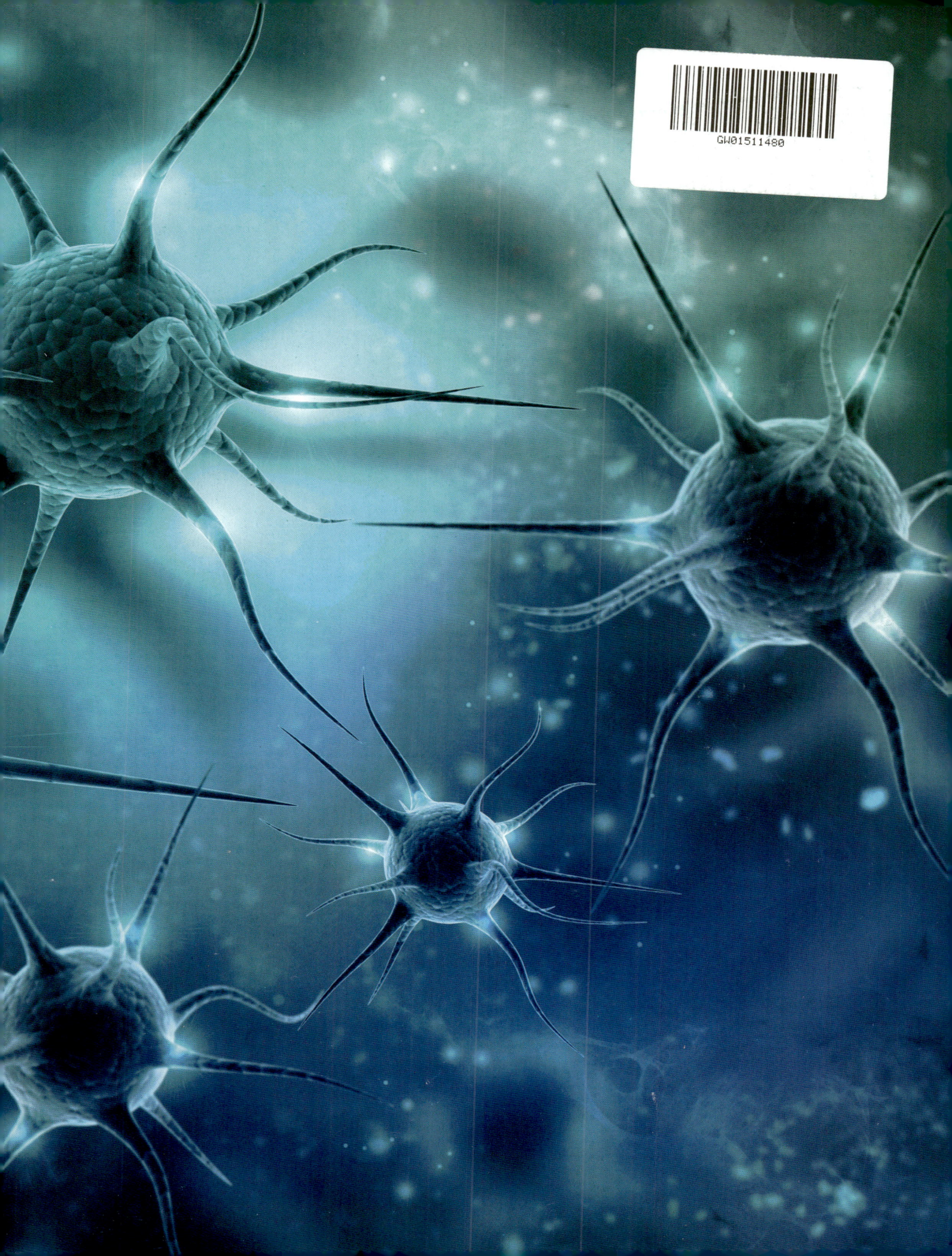

DISCOVER
BACTERIA, VIRUSES & PARASITES

Predominant artwork & imagery source:
Shutterstock.com

Copyright: North Parade Publishing Ltd.

4 North Parade,

Bath,

BA1 1LF, UK

First Published: 2020

All rights reserved. No part of this publication may be reprinted, stored in a retrieval system or transmitted, in any form or by any means, electronic, mechanical, photocopying, recording, or otherwise, without the prior permission of the copyright holder.

Printed in China.